Sex in the Forbidden Zone

SEX
IN THE
FORBIDDEN
ZONE

WHEN MEN IN POWER—
THERAPISTS, DOCTORS,
CLERGY, TEACHERS,
AND OTHERS—
BETRAY WOMEN'S TRUST

PETER RUTTER, M.D.

JEREMY P. TARCHER, INC.
Los Angeles

Excerpts from *The Good Mother* by Sue Miller. Copyright © 1986
by Sue Miller. Reprinted by permission of Harper & Row,
Publishers, Inc.

Library of Congress Cataloging in Publication Data

Rutter, Peter.
  Sex in the forbidden zone : when men in power—therapists,
doctors, clergy, teachers, and others—betray women's trust / Peter
Rutter.
  p. cm.
  Bibliography.
  1. Sexual ethics—United States.   2. Professional employees—
United States—Sexual behavior.   3. Professional ethics—United
States.   I. Title.
HQ32.R87   1989   89-33223
306.7—dc20   CIP
  ISBN 0-87477-486-1
  ISBN 0-87477-487-X (pbk.)

Jeremy P. Tarcher, Inc.
9110 Sunset Blvd.
Los Angeles, CA 90069

Distributed by St. Martin's Press, New York

Manufactured in the United States of America
10 9 8 7 6 5 4 3 2 1

First Edition

For three who graced us with their presence, but
were taken far too early: my mother,
Sylvia Weber Rutter, and my dear friends,
Mel Fohrman and Stephen Walters

Contents

Let us remember: What hurts the victim most is not the cruelty of the oppressor, but the silence of the bystander.

—ELIE WIESEL

I swear by Apollo the physician and by Aesculapius to keep the following oath: I will prescribe for the good of my patients and never do harm to anyone. In every house where I come I will enter only for the good of my patients, keeping myself far from all intentional ill-doing and all seduction, and especially from the pleasures of love with women or men, be they free or slaves.

—FROM THE HIPPOCRATIC OATH

Acknowledgments

Enduring thanks to Donald Sandner, John Beebe, Spiro Kostof, Jean Bolen, Jonathan Harris, Joel Braziller, Robert Caserio, Lynn Franco, Margaret Skinner, John Steiner, Richard Hutson, Dennis Turner, and William McGuire, for encouraging me when this project was in its fragile early stages and for their sustained wise counsel along the way.

To Camille LeGrand, Loren Pedersen, Teresa Bernardez, Jeffrey Kottler, Jane Vinson, Nadine Taub, Cari Lenahan, and Gary Schoener, for graciously sharing with me their trailblazing work in a way that allowed me to do my own.

To Jean Naggar, my literary agent, for being there first, last, and always. To my editor, Connie Zweig, who became an alchemical *soror mystica*; and to my publisher, Jeremy Tarcher, who as symbolic father was a steadfast source of help and hope. No author could have asked for a team that bestowed more depth, relationship, and hard work.

But most of all to my wife, Virginia Beane Rutter, and to our children, for their unfaltering patience and love.

A Personal Note

Twenty years ago I began my psychiatric practice with the unchallenged belief that having sex with my patients was completely out of the question. I accepted with a naive faith the presence of impermeable sexual boundaries as a prerequisite to the doctor-patient relationship that had existed since the days of Hippocrates nearly 2,500 years ago.

I assumed that everyone in my professional community also observed this prohibition. The only doctors and therapists who had sexual relations with patients were, I was sure, confined to the criminal or lunatic fringe, such as the surgeon who sexually assaulted his female patients after placing them under anesthesia, or the occasional therapist who would establish a "therapeutic" commune conveniently populated by women willing to be his sexual partners.

It took me nearly a decade to stop believing in the myth of the beneficent doctor. I discovered instead that sexual exploitation by men of women under their care or tutelage is not unusual and in actuality is quite common. Furthermore, I found remarkably similar patterns of sexual contact not only by male doctors and therapists but by male clergy, lawyers, teachers, and workplace mentors. These highly eroticized entanglements can occur, behind closed doors, in any relationship in which a woman entrusts important aspects of her physical, spiritual, psychological, or material welfare to a man who has power over her.

I also found that the men who have sex with their female patients, clients, parishioners, students, and protégées are not the obviously disturbed men who occasionally show up in the

1

headlines. Instead, they are accomplished professionals, admired community leaders, and respectable family men whose integrity we tend to take for granted. I can now see that sexual violation of trust is an epidemic, mainstream problem that reenacts in the professional relationship a wider cultural power-imbalance between men and women.

This radical shift in my outlook was shaped by a personal involvement in two highly charged, interrelated episodes. The first, a near-sexual encounter with a woman patient, forced me to acknowledge the side of myself that yearned for just such a forbidden episode. It made me confront the degree to which my own fantasy life becomes activated in my work, and it led me to uncover the reasons even ethical men tend to condone silently the sexual misdeeds of their less ethical colleagues.

The second episode, the disclosure that a psychiatrist who had been my mentor and role model had for years engaged in sex with many of his women patients, shattered my naiveté so profoundly that I felt compelled to look as deeply as I could into this problem as a way of reshaping my sense of reality. Out of this investigation came answers about to be presented to the mystery of why so many men and women collude in sexually exploitative behavior, in and out of professional circumstances.

MY ENCOUNTER WITH MIA

The first episode came upon me suddenly, dangerously, in the closed chamber of my first psychiatric office, when I felt the psychological barriers protecting me from forbidden sexuality come tumbling down. It happened on a dark, rainy evening in early December when a patient I will call Mia came to her usual appointment with the unspoken, unplanned, but extremely compelling agenda to offer herself to me sexually.

Mia was a tall, dark-haired woman of twenty-five whose

brightly colored clothes and quick pace masked her severe chronic depression. Her quest for happiness persisted despite the fact that life had dealt her almost nothing but deprivation and loss. Both of her parents had recently passed away after recurrent bouts with depression and alcoholism, and she had an older brother about whom she had hazy memories of possible sexual molestation. After drifting into street life and drug abuse in her late teens, Mia was trying to put her life together. She was off drugs, working as a receptionist for a plastic surgeon, and developing an interest in psychology.

During the five months she had been my patient, Mia and I had identified her pattern of becoming sexually intimate with men rather quickly because she felt she had no other way to keep them interested. Nevertheless, she had never been in the least bit seductive with me. But without warning, that night I felt her sexuality directed toward me from the moment she stepped into the room—with an intensity beyond anything I had yet experienced in the seven years I had been practicing psychiatry.

Mia made her way to the patient's chair, but she did not stay there. As she spoke, tearfully recounting a humiliating rejection she had suffered the day before with a man she had been dating, she gradually slid off the chair onto the floor and sat cross-legged in front of me. The sexual posturing in her behavior grew more intense as she pleadingly looked up at me, wondering through her tears whether men would always use her up and throw her away. In her desperate need for comfort, Mia began to edge her way toward me, brushing her breasts against my legs, beginning to bury her head in my lap. As she inexorably reenacted her familiar role as sexual victim, all she needed to complete it was my participation.

My likelihood of collaborating in this sexual scenario was enhanced by the fact that, because of losses in my own personal life, I had been feeling quite depressed that winter, and I had no place to go that evening except back to the empty house where I lived alone. Mia was the last patient on my schedule. It had long since become dark outside, and as we sat in my warm office listening to the cold rain outside, I knew that we were the only ones left in the office building.

Nothing in my training had prepared me for this moment. As Mia moved closer to me, I sat frozen, neither encouraging nor stopping her. I was overcome by an intoxicating mixture of the timeless freedom, and the timeless danger, that men feel when a forbidden woman's sexuality becomes available to them. The freedom stems from the illusion of such moments in which a man can convince himself that nothing but sexual merger with the female body and spirit seems real. He shuts himself off from past and future, contemplating neither his motivation nor the consequences of his acts. The feeling of danger balances the one of freedom, for within this danger is the intuition that the act he is so strongly fantasizing may be wrong, that it may bring catastrophe on both himself and the woman. In the moment of deciding whether to cross this line, I felt all at once extremely powerful—and very, very vulnerable.

Another part of me, however, remained completely separate from this sexual intrigue, disbelieving that erotic contact between us could be imminent. This part, the detached professional, was trying to understand what was going on inside Mia and searched for a way to help her; he knew that sexual contact could not under any circumstances be allowed. But another part of me—the generic man with a standard masculine fantasy-life—had been well coached by his culture to accept as good fortune the sexual opportunity being proffered.

I knew that by doing nothing at all, I could simply allow Mia to touch me in what was certainly going to be a sexual way. I could passively accede to her agenda, letting my depression mirror her own, allowing us to become wounded patients together. I sensed that if I went ahead with this sexual encounter, I would be able to count on Mia to keep our illicit secret. As a well-trained victim, she would most likely refuse to see my sexual behavior as an abusive act: She would agree, if I asked it of her, to believe that sexual contact could be a legitimate part of our therapy; or she would conspire with me to pretend afterward that it had never occurred. In any event, it was extremely unlikely that I would have to answer to anybody if I proceeded.

I made a choice in that moment, one that my more opportunistic side has at times regretted: I asked Mia to return to her chair. She did so without hesitation, as if a healthier part of her was poised for this precise request. In our respective seats, we were able to begin a therapeutic exploration of the way, in her blind search for a man's comforting warmth, she had repeatedly offered herself sexually to men. By my not complying with her seductive behavior, we were able to talk about it. After all, Mia had just done exactly what patients are supposed to do when they see their doctors: She was bringing me her illness, her self-destructive pattern, in the only way she knew how—by repeating it with me, right there in the room. Along with her hunger for warmth and affection, she was showing me that she had always been out of control of her own sexual boundaries.

I realized during this episode that I could either have victimized her as others had, or I could offer her a way to begin recovering from her past injuries. At this critical moment, the path taken depended not on her but entirely on me. In order to steer her toward the healthy side, I had to fight off some typically masculine components of my sexuality that were all too ready to accept Mia's self-destructive offering. I still shudder to think how close I came to harming the two of us.

From this experience I discovered at first hand just how passionate and dissolving the erotic atmosphere can become in relationships in which the man holds the power and the woman places trust and hope in him. Any illusion I had that I was exempt from this seductive intensity was left far behind. It was suddenly clear to me that having sex with patients was not out of the question at all. In fact, it was both more readily possible and powerfully alluring than I had ever admitted to myself.

The allure of the forbidden is a central theme not only of this book but of male sexual psychology. It is present in the therapist's office and in any relationship of trust in which a man holds power over a woman's intimate aspirations.

Day after day, we men sit in inviolable privacy with women who trust, admire, and rely upon us. There is a constant pull toward greater intimacy. Businessmen travel with their female protégées, sharing long hours in airplanes and adjacent lodgings in far-away cities. Women who see lawyers, especially in divorce or custody cases, usually disclose to them the most intimate details of their lives, including a history of their sexual behavior. A male teacher in high school, college, or graduate school can invite a woman's trust through his ability to foster her intellectual, professional, or spiritual development. A doctor has instantaneous access to a woman's unclothed body. When a woman sees a male physician she yields to him her most private physical being along with the psychological sense of self she experiences through her body. Therapists and clergy invite the women under their care to share secrets, sexual and otherwise, disclosed to no one else, without regard to social propriety or rationality.

These women make good on our invitations to intimacy, bringing us long-hidden feelings, dreams, and fantasies. These feelings, often laced with passions both luminous and dark, swirl about the room. In a mysterious way, almost like electromagnetic induction, we men cannot stop ourselves from beginning to experience, prompted by what women share with us, some of our own long-denied fears, injuries, hopes, and fantasies. Just as the woman in a relationship of trust may look to the man in power for an answer to what has been injured or unfulfilled in her, the man may begin to look to the woman as a source of healing for himself.

To me, and to all men in power, the woman can easily become a sympathetic, wounded, vulnerable presence who admires and needs us in an especially feminine way. If we have been working together for some time, a familiarity and trust develops between us that starts to erode the boundaries of seemingly impersonal professional relationships. Whether they say so openly or not, these women often convey their feeling that we are treating them far better than they ever dreamed a man could. As a result, we may find ourselves experiencing a closeness, a comfort, a sense of *completeness* with these women that we have long sought but rarely found; many of them clearly begin to feel the same way about being with us.

Under these conditions, images of sexual union flood us. The rule forbidding sexual contact with these women can seem hazy and distant, no longer applicable. We long to be free of the special obligations that prohibit sexual expression of our feelings for each other. In the moment, it feels so easy, so magical, so relieving for us to cross the invisible boundary and merge with the woman in shared passion.

Yet every time I have found myself caught up in sexual fantasies about a patient, I have discovered, as I did that evening with Mia, that something holds me back—not just a rule against sexual contact, but a feeling that something of value, right there in the room, will be destroyed if that line is crossed.

And still I remain ambivalent, as do virtually all of my male colleagues. No matter how well I have learned to recognize and use sexual tensions in a therapeutic, nonphysical way, at times I still feel pulled in by the seductive intimacy of my work. There seems to be nothing I can do to prevent an occasional fantasy of sexual contact with a female patient. And although now I know how my struggle will be resolved, each time I must put forth deliberate effort to remember how and why I must resist the temptation to get out of my chair, traverse the short distance to my patient, and embrace her.

Although it is not permitted by the social rules by which we have agreed to live, forbidden sexual contact remains right there, available and accessible, ours for the taking.

BETRAYAL BY MY MENTOR

The second episode that led me to write this book was the painful and disturbing discovery that a mentor who had seemed to represent all the best qualities of a teacher and healer had been repeatedly making a different choice—having sexual relations with many of his female patients. Dr. Edward Reynolds (as I shall call him) seemed the embodiment of the altruistic, caring psychotherapist. In his late forties, this distinguished, dark-haired man of patrician reserve had a soft, receptive bearing that made him appear wise and accessible to psychotherapists-in-training and, one imagined, to patients as well. He seemed a particularly unselfish man, willing to work with patients who had no money or were considered untreatable by others.

I was one among many younger therapists, both men and women, who considered him a uniquely valuable role model, that special kind of teacher who inspires both outer and inner development. On the outer, practical level he taught us specific skills of psychotherapy; on the inner level he helped awaken in us a personal sense of ethical and creative involvement with our work.

It was against this background of admiration that I heard the first rumor that Dr. Reynolds had been having sexual relationships with his female patients. I distinctly remember watching a nearly impenetrable wall of denial go up inside my mind. The notion of Dr. Reynolds having sex with patients was completely preposterous. He was a man who articulated for the rest of us the most humane values of our profession. No one knew better than he that sexual contact with patients was out of the question because of the clear abuse of power involved and the great harm it caused. He would never betray his values and all he had taught us about the art of healing. It was all, literally, incredible.

But along with my disbelief I was surprised to discover a simultaneous certainty within that what I was hearing *had* to be true. I watched these other thoughts arise, dimly and faintly—as if they belonged to someone else—from beyond my wall of denial, from another place that was willing to accept the truth. Nonetheless, there finally came a time at which at last I could say to myself, "Of *course* he's sleeping with his patients; I have absolutely no doubt about it. It figures; it makes total sense. It explains a lot about him, about how I've felt around him at times."

When we listen to the part of ourselves that has no need to push away the truth, we may feel as if a missing piece of the deeper plan of things has been given to us. And we know that it fits, that it must be true. But there are tremendous pressures from the external world that force us to deny and devalue these more intuitive, inner voices.

In this case, when I heard my intuitive voice I refused to listen; it was just too threatening. Without being aware of it then, I still needed to protect my image of the "good father" in Dr. Reynolds. Reality would have to wait until I was ready to accept it. Unfortunately, as is characteristic of the way we deny when faced with issues of forbidden sexuality, it took me and most of my colleagues years to absorb the truth. In the meantime, tacitly protected by our silence, Dr. Reynolds continued having sex with more patients, creating more damage.

Finally, when enough ex-patients had lodged complaints about his sexual misconduct, a group of silent colleagues and I faced reality and voted to expel him from our professional association. Five years had passed since I had first heard about his sexual exploits with patients; I subsequently discovered that other colleagues had been hearing such stories for more than a decade.

I found it difficult to fathom why nobody, including myself, had done anything to stop this man. It began to dawn on me that the most mysterious dimension of this kind of betrayal might *not* be the fact that a certain number of men would always try to sexually exploit women in relationships of trust; this phenomenon, although unpleasant to acknowledge, is rather understandable. It was far more difficult to understand why so many of us, bystanders and victims alike, had remained silent in the face of these violations.

With this question came the beginning of my task of exploring the role each of us plays in this silent conspiracy. The first place I looked for answers, before I was able to talk to other people about this subject, was inside myself. I already knew that I was capable of having powerful fantasies about sexual contact with patients. I also knew that I had held on to an idealized version of Dr. Reynolds long after I should have.

When I went back to examining my denial of his sexual exploits, I came upon another, even darker dimension of the hidden world of masculine sexual psychology: I realized that whenever I thought about his forbidden liaisons, beneath my outrage lurked a secret envy. I wished I could do what he had done. I heard my inner voices rapidly run the gamut from *Oh, how awful! That terrible man. The deceit. The selfishness . . .* to *How could he do it? How did he carry it off?* How indeed? *What's his secret? If he could do it, why can't I? It's something I've always wished for. Maybe one day I won't have to be so strict about upholding sexual boundaries with my own patients.*

I felt quite alone on first unearthing these secret thoughts that ran in a direction so contrary to that of the ethics of my profession. But when I began gingerly broaching sexual issues with male friends and colleagues, I found that virtually every associate shared similar feelings and experiences. Over the years, each of the hundreds of men I spoke with on this subject admitted that on some level he envied other men's forbidden sexual exploits. The impact of so many men sharing a similar sexual fantasy would turn out to be a key element in explaining why even ethical men look the other way when they hear about a colleague's sexually exploitative behavior.

THE FORBIDDEN ZONE: EVERYWHERE AND NOWHERE

The question of how easily well-respected men of power could repeatedly sexually exploit women without ever being discovered left me both disturbed and fascinated. I felt I had to learn as much as I could about how and why this happened, about how women felt about having sex with their doctors, teachers, or therapists, about the wider social and cultural dynamics of this problem. I redirected my exploration away from my own feelings about this subject back toward the outer world.

At this stage, I found a phrase—"sex in the forbidden zone"—to describe any sexual contact that occurred within professional relationships of trust. I discovered that sex in the forbidden zone was, in a sense, nowhere and everywhere at the same time. It was practically nowhere to be found in books or in the professional literature (an issue I will take up more fully in the next section as a symptom of how hard our culture works to suppress and deny the problem of sexual misconduct by men in power). Yet as I began talking with people—friends, acquaintances, colleagues, patients—I found that sex in the forbidden zone was everywhere, especially in the experience of women.

Remarkably, once invited to talk about it, women were not at all reticent in sharing their stories. Almost 80 percent of the women I spoke with had an incident to recount about having been approached sexually by a man who was her doctor, therapist, pastor, lawyer, or teacher. In about half of the cases, an actual sexual relationship took place, with disastrous results. Those who did not become sexually involved reported feeling outraged, confused, or sickened by the man's erotic innuendos in ways that forever compromised a once-vital relationship. The 20 percent of women to whom this had never happened all knew two or three other women to whom it had.

Moreover, no group of women seemed to be exempt based on level of education or professional development. I discovered this when I consulted several leading female attorneys and therapists for their help in understanding this problem from a woman's perspective and in locating subjects I could interview for my research. I was shocked when so many of these highly competent, professional women eventually revealed to me that they, too, had had past sexual involvements with male professors, therapists, or mentors. This experience forced me to abandon forever the illusion that sex in the forbidden zone is a small, circumscribed problem limited to a few less-principled men interacting with a few especially vulnerable women.

Although I will review the few studies that have attempted measurement of the incidence of this problem using statistical methods, this is an issue whose scope thus far defies statistical analysis. Women who participate in forbidden-zone sex tend to be too ashamed or afraid to reveal it. And the percentage of men willing to admit to their own sexual misconduct is minuscule.

Fortunately, there is another way to measure and study reality, one that long predates our servitude to numbers: It is called "asking around." I invite you to try it. If you do, chances are that you will hear, within one or two instances of asking the question, about one woman, then another and another, who had a sexual relationship with a man who had power over her. Once you start piecing together all of these stories, it becomes clear from the experience of women that sexual exploitation of professional relationships is epidemic in our society.

Aside from the enormous prevalence of this problem, other interesting patterns began to emerge as my network of information grew. At first I researched only sexual relationships between male therapists and female patients. This was the world I knew best—the one in which I had experienced both alluring danger with my patient Mia and confusing disillusion through my mentor's fall from grace. But when I told women that my interest lay not only in the external facts but also in the psychological dynamics between a man and woman that would permit these sexual relationships to occur, many told me about other kinds of relationships—with pastors, lawyers, and teachers—in which they felt that their trust had been exploited in ways that appeared identical to that which occurred between therapists and patients.

The pattern of sexual betrayal of trust widened still further when some women told me that they had felt the same kind of sexual pressure on the job. I had not been looking for this pattern in the workplace. Sexual harrassment is somewhat different from sex in the forbidden zone because it can occur between a woman and a coworker or boss with whom she has no special relationship or reason for trust.

The configuration I was studying, on the other hand, had as a central factor the existence of a relationship of trust that was betrayed through sexual behavior. Nevertheless, many women told me that they had, indeed, developed relationships of trust at work with male mentors who were more than just bosses or supervisors. When they described the effect on them of a sexual innuendo, demand, or consummated relationship with such a mentor, it contained the central forbidden-zone theme of betrayal of what had been a *nonsexual* relationship with a man who had been centrally important to a woman's development. I realized that as more women enter the workplace in increasingly sophisticated jobs, the problem of sex between mentor and protégée was becoming increasingly prevalent and needed to be addressed and understood in terms of its underlying psychology.

I began to see that what I was calling sex in the forbidden zone had, under various terms that addressed different aspects of this phenomenon, always been of great interest to the public through the media attention given, for example, to incidents of sexual misconduct by pastors and politicians both famous and obscure. Whether it was a local clergyman who was being reprimanded or discharged for having sexual relations with a single congregant, or wider-scale sexual exploitation by spiritual or religious leaders, some of whom formed cultlike communities, many stories began to find their way through the veil of secrecy into the headlines. In all of these incidents, the underlying dynamics of abuse sounded remarkably similar, regardless of the religion involved—whether the exploitation took place in mainstream Protestant and Catholic churches, American Buddhist communities, or television ministries with a show-business aura, such as the one headed by the Reverend Jim Bakker.

In addition to the Jim Bakker–Jessica Hahn scandal, the events that caused Gary Hart to withdraw from the presidential race were widely publicized during the research stage of this book. Although neither one fit into the classic forbidden-zone pattern that I was beginning to identify, these two sexually tinged episodes that caught the public's interest raised enough questions about sexual behavior by powerful men to seem relevant to the subject at hand.

The incident with the strongest impact on our political history, because it ended the candidacy of a man who was in a strong position to become President, was the revelation of the Gary Hart–Donna Rice relationship. We do not know whether Gary Hart betrayed Donna Rice's trust, because we have no information about the psychological circumstances of their meeting. We do know that as a charismatic national figure Senator Hart had enormous personal power in relation to Ms. Rice, and that he cut off their relationship as soon as it became public. Although she may not perceive herself to be a victim, Donna Rice stands as a cultural symbol of the woman who is sexually used by a powerful man until she no longer suits his purposes, at which point she is cast out of his life.

Whether he betrayed her trust or not, we do know that Senator Hart betrayed ours. Much as we may get used to the idea that men in power may have secret sexual lives, we also somehow expect better of them, and we are injured whenever we discover that our better hopes have been betrayed. Although President John F. Kennedy successfully concealed his sexual double life from the public when he held office, many people feel quite differently about him, and about the hope his graceful public image engendered, now that his private life has been more thoroughly revealed.

In a sense, we as a nation enter into forbidden-zone relationships of trust with our leaders. They have enormous power over our lives, and they become perforce our guides or spiritual leaders and potential healers on a societal level. Different men violate this trust in different ways, not only through their sexual behavior. But deep down, we seem to know when we are betrayed.

From both the mass media and from a growing personal research network, more and more detailed evidence of sexual exploitation by men in power began to come my way, some through the phenomenon of "Everybody Knows" stories. When people cross a certain threshold into a subject that was once taboo, a dramatic switch to great openness can occur. All of a sudden I began hearing such things as "Everybody knows that divorce lawyers are notorious for becoming sexually involved with their female clients," and "When I was in graduate school in psychology, everyone knew that it was routine for the female students to sleep with their dissertation advisers." The Everybody Knows phenomenon would at times single out an individual about whom "everybody knows that he sleeps with his patients [or clients, or students, or protégées]."

This stage of research was a welcome and constructive compensation for the well-guarded silence that I had originally encountered. This sudden flood of information revealed that beneath our denial we really know a great deal about forbidden-zone sex and find it freeing to learn that others have already begun to speak out. Although the Everybody Knows approach carries a risk of spreading unfounded rumors about people, when it comes to sex in the forbidden zone, what Everybody Knows vastly underestimates the truth.

Despite reluctance to acknowledge the existence of a forbidden zone, it turns out that many people know it exists and sense that it is being violated on an enormous scale, day in and day out. Although statisticians would blanch at the statement "It happens all the time!" I began hearing this phrase quite frequently as a companion to "Everybody knows."

Finally, in the course of my inquiries, I started interviewing in depth and detail the men and women whose first-person accounts of sex in the forbidden zone inform this book. In listening to them, I did not wonder for a moment if what these people were saying was true, for I knew it was. I did not conduct a structured interview, with preset questions and categories of information. I simply sat and spoke with these men and women, often for hours on end. Several interviews were by long-distance telephone, and I have never met face-to-face some of the people who related their painful experiences. Their words offer not quantitative truth but unalloyed and highly intimate emotional truth.

For many I interviewed, talking about their forbidden-zone sexual relationships was a new experience. Thus, many of them, as we spoke, had their first chance in the years since to reflect upon the impact of these sexual involvements. Sadly, most of these women were still dealing with discovering how extensively damaging these experiences had been—whether one or twenty years had passed. I was wisely instructed and deeply moved with each of them.

I was learning more than I had expected about sexual exploitation and seeing it in places I had never thought to look. The key elements in the way a man in power sexually exploited a woman's trust seemed to be virtually identical, whether the man was called a doctor, psychiatrist, psychologist, therapist, professor, mentor, priest, minister, rabbi, or guru. The difficulty a woman has in saying no to sexual contact was similar in all those relationships. All the forbidden sexual liaisons took place in an atmosphere of enforced silence, which was observed not only by the men and women who became involved but also by witnesses who did nothing to stop it. I know, because I too had been a silent bystander.

Prologue

Mapping the Territory:
Terminology, Statistics, and Sources

This book is about why men and women have so much trouble keeping sexuality out of relationships where it does not belong, and about why fantasies of sexual contact with forbidden partners often have an irresistible allure. It is based on my experience as a psychiatrist with the dangerous mixture of sexuality and power that develops when women sit down behind closed doors with their male doctors, psychotherapists, clergymen, lawyers, teachers, and mentors.

Although such relationships are meant to serve protective, nonsexual purposes, they often become intensely erotic, offering up intoxicating fantasies of sexual merger to the man in power, to the woman whose intimate trust he holds, or to them both. Despite the fact that men have moral, legal, and ethical responsibilities not to allow themselves to become sexually involved with their female patients, clients, parishioners, students, and protégées, there is a largely concealed epidemic, affecting over one million men and women, of exploitative sexual contact in violation of this forbidden boundary.

Both men and women readers will recognize that the lessons of the forbidden zone apply far beyond the professional consulting room to sexual boundary tensions we experience daily in public places, in the workplace, and with colleagues and friends. In addition, this description of sex in the forbidden zone should lend new insights to related problems such as rape, incest, child molestation, sexual harassment, date rape, adultery, and sexual addiction, all of which share many of the psychological and cultural dynamics underlying sexual exploitation by professionals.

This book applies both psychological and cultural perspectives concerning sexuality to show how large-scale social forces incite both men and women to reenact abusive patterns with one another. Although women are the obvious victims of forbidden-zone exploitation, men in power also victimize themselves through destructive expressions of sexuality, leaving untouched the wounds that lie hidden beneath their inappropriate sexual behavior. The damage caused by betrayal of intimate trust, in or out of the forbidden zone, is severe.

Because 96 percent (a consensus figure based on studies that have been done) of sexual exploitation by professionals occurs between a man in power and a woman under his care, and because the male-female power imbalance is reflective of the pattern that exists in the culture at large, the forbidden zone defined in this book concerns men in power who exploit women. Although women in power can also exploit men, and although both men and women engage in homosexual exploitation, such situations represent a small percentage of cases of professional abuse.

In some way, sex in the forbidden zone touches and wounds us all. Women are accustomed to being its victims, discovering again and again that few relationships with men can be considered safe from sexual demand. Even if sex never takes place, a woman must deal with a pressure that is expressed by a covert nuance of speech, a carelessness of a man's touch, a subtle steering of a relationship in directions that serve the man's sexual aims.

If this man is important to her—as her mentor, her boss, her therapist, her pastor, even her friend or coworker—she may try to overlook the sexual element or even begin to cater to it, for fear of losing a relationship of value. Yet I have found

that when a woman makes *any* compromise with inappropriate sexual expression from a man, she yields control over her
own intimate boundaries and begins a dangerous collaboration that can lead to her victimization.

For victimization it is. Because men so often control access
to a woman's future—and to her physical, psychological, spiritual, economic, or intellectual well-being—the mere presence
of sexual innuendo from a man who has power over her can
become a barrier to her development. But the most critical
damage lies in the silencing of her own voice and the violation
of her sense of self. Presented in these pages is the feminine
experience of sex in the forbidden zone through the stories of
women who participated in it. Explained too are the underlying fantasies and dynamics of feminine sexual psychology
that hold women to such involvements despite the damage.

My position is that *any sexual behavior by a man in power
within what I define as the forbidden zone is inherently exploitative of a woman's trust.* Because he is the keeper of that
trust, it is the man's responsibility, *no matter what the level of
provocation or apparent consent by the woman,* to assure that
sexual behavior does not take place.

On the other hand, when a man who has power over and
intimate access to a woman maintains complete respect for
her sexual boundaries, the healing promise of relationships of
trust between men and women can be fulfilled. Instances of
the hopeful side of forbidden-zone relationships, the healing
moments that can occur when a man in power relinquishes
his view of a woman as a potential sexual partner, will also be
explored in the pages to come.

Men's cultural training, often reinforced by family messages when they are growing up, encourages them to challenge women's intimate boundaries and discourages them
from developing a more empathic response to the feminine,
despite the fact that they have so much more to offer women
than predatory sexual opportunism.

Because for men sexuality is often most intense when it is
most forbidden, the fact that a man holds a position of trust

in itself offers no protection from the possibility that he will push toward sexual contact. The ordinary man, with an inclination to cross over forbidden boundaries, emerges from beneath the professional role.

The damage a man causes himself when he violates these boundaries is often elusive, because in the moment of forbidden sex he may be able to convince himself that he is satisfying a deeply felt need. Yet in the very act of exploiting the woman in order to feel more fully alive, he abandons the search for aliveness within himself. When a man's brief moment of forbidden sexual release is over, he is left with more emptiness than before. He is farther still from the access to resources within himself that his sexual fantasy represents, and he is in denial of his own psychological wounds.

These wounds, for reasons soon to be explained, imbue fantasies of sexual contact with forbidden partners with stunningly erotic qualities, adding to the difficulty men have with sexual boundaries. But when these boundaries can be respected, men can gain access to inner resources to replace the feeling that the only way to heal their wounds is through sexual contact with women.

This book explains the reasons that forbidden sexuality is so alluring to men; shows how women collaborate in allowing themselves to be sexually exploited; and describes the cultural and psychological wounds to both men and women that pave the way for involvement in destructive sexuality. Along with instances of the severe damage caused by sex in the forbidden zone, I also suggest measures one can take to recover from and prevent exploitative sex.

NAMING THE UNNAMEABLE

SEX IN THE FORBIDDEN ZONE: Sexual behavior between a man and a woman who have a professional relationship based on trust, specifically when the man is the woman's doctor, psychotherapist, pastor, lawyer, teacher, or workplace mentor.

In order to break through the complex psychological and cultural curtain of silence protecting men in power who abuse women's trust, the syndrome had to be named in its broadest context. Our attempts to understand the darker corners of the human condition are significantly impeded when we lack a vocabulary with which to name the damaging ways people treat one another.

Historically, many practices that we consider to be grievous moral wrongs, such as rape, slavery, and genocide, have been, in certain times and in certain cultures, completely acceptable. These wrongs, despite being widespread, remained unnamed and invisible, a tribute to how fully integrated they were into the fabric of social life.

Identifying a mode of behavior by giving it a name with negative connotations is one of the earliest signs that some members of a society are beginning to challenge the acceptability of that behavior. Words like *racism, sexism,* and *ageism* are coinages of the twentieth century that have emerged as society became capable of identifying these practices as unjust and reformable elements of our culture's standard operating procedure. It is impossible to pass a law against something that you cannot name.

Even the term *sexual harassment,* now so conspicuously in the public vocabulary, began to be used in its current meaning only as recently as 1976. One can imagine women in the workplace before then searching to describe how they were being treated, trying to find a way to express the feeling that they no longer wanted to accept this treatment as "normal."

And in some quarters, sexual exploitation of women by therapists was until recently widely considered to be fabricated. If a woman made such a claim, she was often dismissed as having fantasized it, or she was blamed as the alleged seductress. Dr. Alan A. Stone, a leading scholar on psychiatry and the law, summarizes this attitude in his 1984 book *Law, Psychiatry, and Morality*:

> Twenty years ago female patients who claimed that they had been sexually exploited by their psychotherapists were apt to be written off as having psychotic transferences. The presumption, derived from psychodynamic theories, that these reports represented hysterical wish-fulfilling fantasies, was applied even to victims of rape and incest. Today . . . our former views seem shocking and inexcusable.

The phrase *sex in the forbidden zone,* as defined in this book, brings together with a psychological focus exploitative behaviors that have previously gone by a variety of names. *Sexual misconduct, sexual exploitation, sexual contact, sexual-boundary violation,* and *undue familiarity* are the most common terms currently used to name sexual contact between men in power and women under their care.

Yet distinguishing a sexually forbidden zone from the range of acceptable sexual behavior still needs to be done in many quarters of our society, even among those areas with the highest professional and intellectual sophistication. For instance, more than half of the women interviewed for this book did not know at the time of their sexual contact with a man in power that there are actually ethical standards, and in some cases criminal laws, prohibiting such involvement. These rules and guidelines are summarized in chapter 6.

It is a common practice for men who violate the forbidden zone to tell their female victims that sexual intimacy constitutes acceptable behavior. Most men know better and in saying this are being callously manipulative. But if some men sincerely believe that sex under these conditions is permissible, a sharper definition of relationships in which sexual behavior is inherently damaging is clearly necessary.

The forbidden zone is a condition of relationship in which sexual behavior is prohibited because a man holds in trust the intimate, wounded, vulnerable, or undeveloped parts of a woman. The trust derives from the professional role of the man as doctor, therapist, lawyer, clergy, teacher, or mentor, and it creates an expectation that whatever parts of herself the woman entrusts to him (her property, body, mind, or spirit) must be used solely to advance her interests and will not be used to his advantage, sexual or otherwise.

Under these conditions, sexual behavior is always wrong, no matter who initiates it, no matter how willing the participants say they are. In the forbidden zone, the factors of power, trust, and dependency remove the possibility of a woman freely giving consent to sexual contact. Put another way, the dynamics of the forbidden zone can render a woman unable to *withhold* consent. And because the man has the greater power, the responsibility is his to guard the forbidden boundary against sexual contact, no matter how provocative the woman.

The forbidden zone always exists in the relationship between doctor and patient, therapist and client, clergyman and congregant, lawyer and client, teacher and student. All of these professions carry a special trust not to abuse the seen or unseen dependent elements that inevitably develop. While therapists and pastors deal more overtly with psychological or spiritual injuries, lawyers, teachers, and mentors often deal with the same injuries expressed as outer rather than inner dilemmas. Because its definition rests as much on inner qualities of relationship as on what is visible, the forbidden zone also can arise in other contexts, such as in the workplace, whenever there is inequality of power and the enforced dependency this inequality creates.

In its broadest sense, the sexual forbidden zone can exist in any human relationship in which one person holds power over another, and the purpose of their relating can only be undermined by sexual behavior between them. Many relationships between men and women, even when there is no recognizable ethical barrier against sex, contain hidden power dynamics through which men psychologically coerce women into having sex.

One advantage of demarcating a sexual forbidden zone is that it allows us to identify relationships that have a potential for boundary violations *before* such violations occur. By recognizing in advance that certain configurations of relationship *invite* sexuality at the same time as they *forbid* its expression, we gain options that include prevention of damaging behavior. Given the way our culture encourages men to push against sexual boundaries, *any relationship whatsoever* of unequal power between a man and a woman should be thought of as an arena for possible sexual-boundary violations. Intimate relationships of trust are especially vulnerable to boundary abuse because they invite both men and women to pour into them their strongest hopes, wishes, fantasies, and passions.

Let us look for a moment at the delicate balance between power and trust. Because of the power imbalance in our society, a man often has the key to a woman's career, health, and future. If there is any legitimacy to this power, it must be wielded in trust as part of an ancient moral bargain that endows men—fathers, teachers, physicians, religious, economic, and political leaders—with such authority. A man in a position of power over a woman holds a sacred trust to guard her welfare, guide her safely into life in the wider world, and eventually share the power with her so that she can, if she wishes, leave him and go her own way. When a woman is in the position of power, she, too, holds this responsibility. Today, however, the imbalance is all too frequently in the other direction.

There can be terrible, life-shattering consequences to a girl or woman when this trust is turned into a sexual opportunity by the man in authority. He binds her to him, and when he relinquishes her she is often too injured to find happiness in another relationship. She is likely to adapt to the victim role, repeating it in other relationships, each time losing more of her self-respect and enthusiasm for life.

How a woman is treated in relationships of trust can make the difference between whether she experiences her femininity as a force to be valued and respected or as a commodity to be exploited. Sexual violation of the forbidden zone can kill off hope itself.

SEX IN THE FORBIDDEN ZONE: THE PARTICIPANTS

That the forbidden zone excludes sex between doctors or therapists and their patients has been clearly stated thus far in this introductory material. This section further delineates the reasons why the same prohibitions also apply to pastor-congregant, attorney-client, teacher-student, and workplace-mentor–protégée relationships.

Pastor-Congregant or Clergyman-Parishioner Relationships

I use "clergyman" and "pastor" generically for male religious leaders of any faith, even if that faith has leaders referred to by other names—minister, priest, rabbi, father, or patriarch. The most likely occurrence of the forbidden-zone relationship in a religious setting is in ongoing one-to-one meetings between a clergyman and a woman in his congregation, whether or not these meetings actually consist of pastoral counseling. Although religious and spiritual issues may provide the original motivation for these meetings, more intimate personal matters soon become involved.

The power of the pastor over the congregant is tremendously enhanced by his authority, if he wishes to exercise it, to describe to a woman her status with God. A sexually abusive clergyman can easily exploit this authority by telling a woman that her sexual involvement is part of a divinely ordained plan. Even sophisticated women can have difficulty resisting this argument if they are devoted to the religious vision that the clergyman represents.

Religious cults in which the guru or spiritual leader has sexual relationships with many of his female congregants are more blatant examples of this phenomenon. The leader exploits the trust and value of the spiritual relationship in the same way that therapists, lawyers, teachers, and mentors do in the privacy of their offices.

Attorney-Client Relationships

At first glance, the attorney-client relationship does not necessarily invite the level of trust and intimacy that is so central to the medical, psychotherapeutic, or pastoral relationships. Legal issues revolve around outer, material considerations rather than the realm of feelings or spirit. Nevertheless, there are several reasons why the attorney-client relationship is subject to the sexual prohibitions of the forbidden zone.

First, we must consider the emotional impact of how outer-world problems are resolved to measure how centrally important the attorney-client relationship can be. The result of a legal proceeding can either crush or heal the spirit to the same degree as relationships that deal more directly with inner events. Second, the power dynamics are the same as in other forbidden-zone relationships, and they evoke in women the same psychological vulnerabilities.

Third, many sexual liaisons between attorney and client take place with family lawyers who take divorce and child-custody cases. Family law cases involve the possibility of a woman losing her home, her economic base, and even her relationship with her children. The attorney holds enormous power over the woman's future in situations in which she is faced with the threat of unbearable loss and suffering. The fact that lawyers are not as well trained as therapists in the field of human emotions can increase the sexually abusive potential of this inequality of power.

Teacher/Professor–Student Relationships

My use of the word *teacher* begins with the traditional role of the classroom teacher in the educational system. From the time girls start school as children and go through high school, college, and graduate school, male teachers are usually powerful figures in their lives. Girls and women, through relationships with these teachers, often come to grips with central life issues such as their career identity and their romantic, ethical, and spiritual aspirations. A woman's sense of place in the masculine world is strongly influenced by the degree to which her talent and potential have been recognized by male teachers. Many women report the life-changing influence of one particular teacher. Such influence clearly can be for good or for ill, depending on whether he used his power in an exploitative or respectful way.

The teacher-student relationship can easily develop out of the classroom into a highly individualized one that may take on the aspects of surrogate parenting. This factor underscores the necessity of maintaining a sexual forbidden zone. Although the parenting analogy is more visible when a girl is in elementary or high school, these themes continue as psychological realities throughout a woman's adulthood.

The issue of sexual relationships between professors and students draws attention because of their frequency, which can be partially attributed to a traditional absence of a clearly demarcated forbidden zone on the college campus. People who argue against such prohibitions usually claim that the women involved are consenting adults and that there is no duty to protect them as there is in therapeutic, pastoral, and lawyer relationships. In a prevalent blame-the-victim climate on college campuses, people claim that female students initiate sexual advances toward their professors in order to further their academic careers.

All of these arguments ignore important social and psychological realities. The social dynamic still places the power in the hands of the teacher or professor. The psychological dynamic is based on the underlying reality of continuing dependency issues, which must be taken into account in assessing the ethics of sexual relationships between female college and graduate students and their professors. Recently, some universities have begun articulating clear policies against faculty-student intimacies that do take the unequal power dynamics into consideration (this is discussed further in chapter 7).

A male teacher assumes a particularly special quality of importance to a girl or woman when she meets him at a religious institution. In these cases, whether layman or clergyman, the teacher has the added power of the religious setting and its faith in combination with the teacher-student relationship. When a man has influence over both a woman's outer identity issues and her inner spiritual issues, the binding can be complete. Some of the most egregious cases of exploitation occur when spiritual, educational, and societal needs of a woman are all served through one powerful man.

Mentor-Protégée Relationships

The term *protégée* means "one who is protected by someone older or more powerful." This states precisely the condition that creates the sexual forbidden zone. Because protégée is French for "a protected woman," it serves well as a generic term for the woman in all forbidden-zone relationships. We might let the meaning inherent in the word remind us that a man always has a duty to protect, not invade, his protégée.

In an educational setting, the mentor-protégée relationship can become a highly individualized outgrowth of the teacher-student bond. It carries with it the implication that the teacher has taken on a special responsibility for the student over time.

In the workplace, a woman may find herself developing an important one-to-one relationship with a man who is her supervisor or boss. The relationship takes on special meaning, often to the man in power as well as the woman. He is part teacher, part confessor, part guide. They may spend many hours, even travel, together. Although the relationship has a nonsexual purpose, fantasies of sexual contact may develop in either mentor or protégée in the same way as they do in psychotherapeutic relationships.

The heightened intimacy and importance accorded to the mentoring relationship firmly establish the presence of a sexual forbidden zone. Although the stated ethics of the workplace rarely prohibit the development of sexual intimacy between mentor and protégée, any attempt to cross this line is likely to create the same kind of damage that occurs when a therapist and patient become sexually intimate.

FORBIDDEN-ZONE RESEARCH

The dearth of literature or articles that existed on sexual exploitation in the professions in 1984, when my research began, was shocking. Hadn't anyone, I wondered, studied the incidence of sexual relations between women and their male doctors, therapists, priests, lawyers, teachers, or mentors, or else analyzed the power dynamics of these relationships? Certainly, very few had written about parallels between these abuses of power and other patterns of sexual abuse outside of these special relationships.

I found only two books. One was a first-person account by a woman who had been sexually exploited by her psychiatrist (*Betrayal,* by Lucy Freeman and Julie Roy). The other, incredibly, was by a psychiatrist who advocated the *benefits* of women having sex with their (male) therapists (*The Love Treatment,* by Martin Shepard). Combing through the professional literature unearthed only a handful of articles about sex between patients and their doctors or therapists, and virtually none about sexual contact between women and men in other professions.

Although what little material I found was valuable, and since that time many more articles and several books on the subject have appeared, I was struck then not by what I found but what I did not. The local university medical library, one of the largest in the world, was missing many of the key articles. When I asked a reference librarian to help me search the professional literature for articles about sex between therapists and patients, she was as surprised as I to discover that the vast, enormously sophisticated computerized search system did not even have an applicable subject heading. The professions, I surmised, seemed more than reluctant to admit that sexual misconduct by their members even existed.

A message was being made clear, one that men and women who had previously tried to investigate the dark side of their professions had encountered: "Let's keep this a secret. Don't talk about it; don't read about it; try not to think about it. Whatever you do, don't write about it any place where too many people will find it. Even if we have to discuss it among ourselves, at all costs keep it from the public."

In 1970, Dr. Charles Dahlberg published in the journal *Contemporary Psychoanalysis* one of the earliest studies in the professional literature about sex between therapists and patients. He describes attempts to suppress his article and relegate it to a journal of limited circulation:

> It is surprising that more has not been written about [sex between therapists and patients]. I should note here that I have had trouble getting this paper accepted by larger

organizations where I had less, but still not inconsidera-
ble, influence. I was told it was too controversial. What
a word for a profession that talked about infantile sexuality and incest in Victorian times. . . . "Too hot to handle" [was] a more likely meaning in this instance.

Dr. Nanette Gartrell, a psychiatrist in San Francisco,
and her colleagues Dr. Judith Herman and Dr. Sylvia Olarte
have done the most thorough and up-to-date research sur-
veying the incidence of sexual contact between psychiatrists
and their patients. They tell the story behind the story in a
chapter entitled "Institutional Resistance to Self-Study: A
Case Report" in one of the new breakthrough books on this
subject, *Sexual Exploitation of Patients by Health Professionals*, edited by Ann W. Burgess and Carol R. Hartman. When
Dr. Gartrell was chair of the American Psychiatric Association's Committee on Women, she proposed a survey of the
incidence of sexual exploitation by psychiatrists as a modest
first step in the effort to bring attention to this problem. But
the association, an organization claiming nearly every American psychiatrist as a member, neither provided funds for
this survey nor allowed it to take place under the association's auspices, citing a fear of adverse publicity. Dr. Gartrell, Dr. Herman, and Dr. Olarte instead went outside the
association and obtained private donations in order to carry
out the study.

I was beginning to see how this kind of suppression mir-
rors the secrecy urged upon all sexual victims. Conversely, the
breaking of silence, the defiance of the code of secrecy, has
become a rallying cry for women and men who are trying to
prevent sexual exploitation by addressing the conditions
under which it thrives. Every speech made, every article and
book written about the events and underlying dynamics of
sexual exploitation render less viable the cloak of protection
it has enjoyed.

Because of the code of silence, statistical research in this field is still in its infancy. Most statistical studies are flawed by their reliance on the few men who are willing to admit to their exploitation, insuring that most violation remains unmeasured. Although a statistical base is being collected in medicine, psychotherapy, and university teaching, studies measuring sexual exploitation by lawyers, clergy, and workplace mentors do not yet exist.

Nonetheless, thanks to a small group of pioneering researchers, a faint light has been kindled in a previously all-dark realm. During the last decade, these workers, mostly women, have braved the blockading efforts of their male colleagues to produce a small core of studies and statistics about sex in the forbidden zone. But even they know that giving this problem a name is far more important than giving it a number.

Studies of sexual contact in universities show, with great consistency, that 20 percent to 30 percent of female students have been approached sexually by their professors. A recent report found that 17 percent of female graduate students in psychology had become sexually intimate with a professor during their training, and that an additional 30 percent turned away unwelcome advances. A colleague told me that at his psychology graduate school it was an open secret, and completely accepted, that nearly every female graduate student was sleeping with her dissertation adviser. Yet nobody reported this. Did anybody think it was noteworthy? Or was this behavior too routine to remark on?

Dr. Jacqueline Bouhoutsos, a psychologist in Los Angeles, has conducted pioneering research on sexual exploitation by psychotherapists of all professional backgrounds (including clinical psychologists, psychiatrists, social workers, and marriage counselors). In order to bypass the reliance on men self-reporting their abuses, she and her colleagues designed studies requesting practicing therapists to report whether they have treated patients who had a sexual relationship with a

previous therapist. Her results show that 70 percent of therapists reported at least one patient who had had such a relationship; 96 percent of these previous therapists were male. Dr.
Kenneth Pope and Dr. Bouhoutsos collected this work in the
valuable 1986 study *Sexual Intimacy Between Therapists and
Patients.*

The study by Dr. Judith Herman (author of *Father-Daughter Incest,* the definitive book on a parallel subject) and her
colleagues showed that of 1,057 male psychiatrists who responded to their questionnaire, 7.1 percent *admitted* to having had sexual contact with a patient. They summarize the
broader issues in their September 1986 article in the *American
Journal of Psychiatry*:

> The Hippocratic Oath and the American Psychiatric As-
> sociation code of ethics explicitly prohibit sexual contact
> between psychiatrist and patient. Nevertheless, some
> psychiatrists do become sexually involved with their pa-
> tients. Although documentation of the extent of the prob-
> lem is limited, the best available data indicate that 6
> percent to 10 percent of psychiatrists have had sexual
> contact with their patients, and that the majority of psy-
> chiatrists have knowledge of such cases but do not inter-
> vene. Although the numbers of malpractice claims and
> complaints before ethics committees and licensing
> boards have increased in recent years, it is generally
> agreed that only a very small fraction of these cases ever
> come to public attention.

In medicine, where the power inequality is obvious and
sexual contact with patients is specifically forbidden by the
Hippocratic Oath, a study in the *American Journal of Psychiatry* stated that 13 percent of physicians reported sexual involvement with patients. Of these, a full 80 percent reported
intimate contact with an average of six patients, supporting

the observation that most men who violate the forbidden zone are so-called repeaters who serially exploit woman after woman.

I could not locate a single published statistical study of sexual misconduct among clergymen. However, colleagues who are knowledgeable in this area believe that its incidence among male clergy exceeds the 10 percent estimate for male psychotherapists.

Even if we use the statistics we have conservatively, the numbers of women affected by sex in the forbidden zone are staggering. Excluding workplace mentors, according to the 1986 report of the Bureau of Labor Statistics, approximately 4 million men in the United States are engaged in the other professions covered by the forbidden zone as defined in this book: physicians, psychotherapists, lawyers, clergymen, and teachers.

If we use the minimum figure of 10 percent of these men who exploit the women under their care, and if we assume that these men each had sexual relations with only one protégée, we arrive at a total number of 400,000 victims. But because the studies show that most men who exploit are repeaters who exploit many women, we can multiply this figure (again conservatively) by three to arrive at the not unreasonable figure of over one million women in this country who have been sexually victimized in relationships of trust.

If we add the innumerable workplace mentor-protégée relationships in which sex takes place, there are likely to be several million more women affected. Seen in this light, it becomes understandable that officials in more than one state have declared sexual exploitation of professional relationships to be "a major public health problem."

The work to bring this problem before the public continues. Three other important books in this field were published in 1989. *Is Nothing Sacred?* by Reverend Marie M. Fortune describes an episode of sexual exploitation by a clergyman. *Sex in the Therapy Hour* presents a case study by an abused patient, Carolyn M. Bates, and Dr. Annette M. Brodsky, a leading psychologist in the field of sexual exploitation. The third book is *Sexual Exploitation in Professional Relationships*, edited by Dr. Glen O. Gabbard. Two other recently published first-person accounts by women who were sexually abused by their psychiatrists are *Therapist* by Ellen Plasil and *A Killing Cure* by E. Walker and T. D. Young.

Unpublished doctoral dissertations by Betsy Belote, Sharon Butler, Linda D'Addario (Durre), and Jane S. Vinson—all of the California School of Professional Psychology—have also contributed a rich background of case studies and vital discussion concerning sexual exploitation by psychotherapists.

Where I have quoted from or otherwise drawn directly on the work of others or their observations, I have given attribution directly in the text. All other observations, formulations, and opinions in this book are my own.

Given the obstacles to researching this issue through statistics, this book draws its conclusions from numerous case reports. My observations are drawn from a database of more than 1,000 case reports of male professionals having sexual relations with their patients, clients, parishioners, and students. These reports come from a number of sources: (1) men and women I have seen in my psychiatric practice during the last sixteen years; (2) men and women who were not my patients but agreed to speak with me about their experience expressly for this book; (3) cases that other professionals—psychiatrists, psychologists, clergy, attorneys, teachers—made available to me from their practices; and (4) case reports in papers given at professional conferences, published in the professional literature, or on public record before the courts or state licensing authorities.

Although it is critically important to remove the cloak of secrecy from sex in the forbidden zone, we must do so in ways that do not further violate the privacy and confidentiality of victims by denying them the right to decide when and with whom to share their stories. Professionals also can exploit their clients and patients by either revealing information without their permission or asking them to agree to release of information under circumstances in which they might not feel free to refuse, an ironic parallel to what occurs when a man suggests a sexual relationship to a woman under his care.

I felt that asking my patients to allow me to use their stories in this book might raise issues of exploitation and fuel the hidden obligation to take care of the therapist that so many patients feel. Therefore, with only one exception, none of the cases I describe involves patients from my own practice or betrays confidential case reports given me by colleagues. The one exception involves a woman I stopped treating many years ago, and whom I felt it would not be appropriate to contact to ask her permission. Although I have wrestled with the question of whether it was right for me to share the material in this book, I finally decided to do so, with her identity well disguised.

The other cases I describe in detail come directly from interviews conducted especially for this book. Some of the people were referred to me by lawyers and therapists; others, including a surprising number of women who are now in the helping professions, contacted me when they heard of my research and offered me their experiences. I have presented these cases with varying degrees of disguise, and some represent composites. All names and identifying details relating to the protagonists—both the professional men and the women with whom they were involved—have been changed in the interests of privacy.

Ultimately, these women and men stand here as representatives of an uncountable totality. Each person whose account I present, and all of those whose stories are still concealed, form the center of ripple effects on others that spread in ever-widening circles: Is this woman the only victim of that sexually exploitative psychiatrist? What was the effect on her children of the depression he made more hopeless, or the divorce he helped provoke? How did the psychiatrist's affair with one patient affect the experience of other women he was treating at the same time? How did it affect his own wife and family?

When a pastor shows himself to have been, over many years, continually violating the same rules against sexual misconduct that he has railed at and even punished others for, how does it affect the religious faith and practice of his congregation? What does it say for his particular religious institution, or for the pastorate itself?

And what about men treated by and taught by other men who sexually exploit women? What attitudes toward women are encouraged? I know men who eventually grew to despise and reject healing or mentoring relationships around which they had built their adult identities when they discovered that these therapists, pastors, or teachers had systematically exploited women protégées. Enraged at such a betrayal, they could not avoid also despising themselves for what they considered their blind allegiance. Other men, of course, find it morally convenient to follow in the footsteps of their exploitative role models. As helpful as the emerging statistics are, no numbers can possibly convey the full human cost of sex in the forbidden zone.

A WORD ON TERMINOLOGY

Psychology is uniquely placed to give people a deeper understanding of their own experience. The richest psychological language is the language of everyday life; technical terms detract from this richness. For this reason, I have avoided the use of psychological jargon as much as possible. Instead of taking technical terms and trying to define them for the layperson, I have tried to take everyday terms and imbue them with the psychological meaning they carry in this book. Nevertheless, I will define here certain psychological terms that have been found to be indispensable to a discussion of sex in the forbidden zone:

Boundaries

Boundaries define who we are—where we leave off and the rest of the world begins, what is ours and not ours, what is intimate and what is separate. Sometimes boundaries are physically recognizable. Certainly our bodies and clothing belong to us, and anyone who touches them or gets closer to us than about two feet is entering the intimate space inside our own boundaries. But we have psychological boundaries as well. Unless we have been taught how to recognize and control these less tangible boundaries, other people can psychologically invade us. Such invasions can be damaging in themselves, and they can make us vulnerable to subsequent sexual invasion. Messages we receive from the family and from the culture when we are children determine the degree to which we feel the power to defend our physical and psychological boundaries. In general, men are taught to challenge sexual boundaries in our culture, and women are taught to accept masculine boundary-challenging as a matter of course.

Sexual Behavior/Invasion/Fantasy

Any physical contact or bodily movement intended to express or arouse erotic interest is *sexual behavior.* Distinctions as to who touched whom, in what way, or on what part of the body are irrelevant when it comes to sex in the forbidden zone, where any touching with erotic interest, including touching oneself, is a violation of the boundary. Even an ostensibly accidental brushing of a woman's body must be considered sexually invasive when a man has arranged, with erotic interest, to be close enough so that this "accident" might occur.

Sexual invasion can occur even when there is no touching of the other person. Masturbatory and other provocative bodily movements have equal standing as real sexual acts—even if no contact with the other person is made—and constitute violation of the forbidden zone just as certainly as actual touching does.

Suggestive speech also should be seen as sexual behavior. The way a man speaks to a woman can in itself become an act of sexual invasion. Even standard comments that men make to women such as "You've got a great body" are both invasive and depersonalizing. Given the psychological atmosphere of the forbidden zone, the invasive power of speech must be seen as a concrete act.

Sexuality can be experienced in noninvasive ways, as a feeling dwelling inside oneself, emanating from another person, or present in the "atmosphere." Because sexuality is prevalent in many situations whether or not we wish it, identifying its presence in oneself or in another *before* it gets acted upon, and then learning that there are other options, is of the utmost importance in preventing sexual violation.

Sexual fantasy is a specific form of sexual feeling that uses inner images of sexual behavior to pursue erotic ends. As long as the line is firmly drawn between imagination and realization, sexual fantasy is not invasive and can potentially be put to constructive use by the person doing the fantasizing. Nonetheless, the danger in the forbidden zone is that the man will blur the boundaries of his fantasy to involve the woman whose interests he is obligated to protect.

It is important to clarify the distinction between forbidden sexual *acts* and sexual *feelings*. It is entirely natural to have sexual feelings and fantasies in any relationship of importance. The ability to avoid acting on these feelings is the central challenge of maintaining respect for sexual boundaries.

Abuse, Power, and Trust

The word *abuse* is derived from "use" and means "a departure from [Latin: ab] the purpose [use]." I can think of no more succinct description of sex in the forbidden zone. Remembering that within the word *abuse* lies a purpose that has been lost can help honor that purpose.

Power, as used in the title of this book, refers to a difference in degree of personal and social freedom between two people that leads to one imposing his will on the other. This will is usually imposed psychologically, but it can also have physical manifestations, such as the development of sexual intimacy. The power differential begins when a person with a specific need looks for help from someone more knowledgeable, trained, or competent. Once the relationship begins, the power to impose the will grows immeasurably, because the more powerful person can threaten to abandon the relationship.

Trust, also as used in the title, refers to the assumption by the person with less power in forbidden-zone relationships that the person with greater power will act in her best interest. This assumption has its inner source in the model of the parent-child relationship. The tendency to trust is reinforced, even invited, by the professions themselves, which have codes of ethics asserting that the interest of the patient, client, student, congregant, or protégée must be held uppermost, and that sexual contact is not permissible. As a practical matter, a great many women in forbidden-zone relationships have no other avenue of mending or developing their lives, so they have no choice but to trust that the man in power will use it to help rather than exploit them.

Psyche, Wounds, Transference, and Self

Psyche is an all-embracing term referring to the totality of our psychological capacities and functioning. Mind, feelings, intellect, dreams, emotion, personality, sense of self, inner voice, imagination, competence, despair, and passion are all properties of the psyche.

This book presumes that all of us carry psychological

wounds, which to a greater or lesser degree we try to heal or soothe through our behavior in everyday life. Some people's wounds are evident in their depressive, self-destructive, or exploitative behavior. Other people bear their wounds so secretly that they give no indication of the depth of their suffering. My work as a healer has led me to become quite optimistic that when people's wounds and their personal and cultural origins are recognized, previously unanticipated opportunities arise for healing even the most severely crippling of them. The following chapter has a more extended description of my point of view about the nature of psychological wounds and the way we try to heal them.

Transference is a term used in psychotherapy for the powerful feelings that patients develop toward their therapists. Transference feelings are in some ways a reexperiencing of past emotional dynamics within the family, but in other ways they look to future possibilities for developing new and healthier emotional dynamics. For example, a patient trying to seduce a therapist may be repeating past injuries but is also most likely searching for a response that will discourage this repetition. The therapist draws these feelings out of clients because of the power he has either to reinjure his patients or to relate to them in a way that will free them from the wounds of the past. Many laws defining professional malpractice recognize the life-and-death power that the transference phenomenon grants the therapist and therefore place an extra responsibility on the therapist not to abuse the transference.

Similar transference dynamics take place in all physician-patient, pastor-congregant, lawyer-client, teacher-student, and mentor-protégée relationships, whether recognized or not. Because of this, the ethics of sexual behavior in all of these forbidden-zone relationships have to be judged in light of the transference.

The *self,* as I use it here, refers to an inner core of worth, knowledge, potential, meaning, and aliveness that supersedes the more outer, socially defined self. We are sometimes

shocked when we hear about the personal suffering of someone who has otherwise attained complete success on the
outer, material level. This can occur when outer achievement
is pursued, because of familial and cultural expectations, with
no relation to the values of the self. Ultimately, it is the inner
sense of self that counts when it comes to determining
whether life feels meaningful or worthwhile. The self can be
deeply wounded, but it is also a source of hope, healing, and
regeneration.

For both the man in power and his protégée, strong issues
of self hang in the balance in the forbidden zone. A man's
tendency to form sexual fantasy in the forbidden zone is an
expression of his search for the aliveness of his own self.
Healing moments in the forbidden zone are generated when
both the man and the woman draw upon qualities of self to
resist destructive boundary violations. On the other hand,
most women who have had exploitative sexual relationships
experience a deep wound to their most inner, sacred sense of
self. This psychological injury—often felt as the death of hope
itself—remains the greatest casualty of sex in the forbidden
zone.

One final point of orientation: My subspecialty as a psychiatrist is Jungian psychoanalysis, in which I have taken post-
graduate training. C. G. Jung, a Swiss psychiatrist, considered
events that occur *inside* the human psyche to be as real, name-
able, and understandable as those we see *outside* us. Many of
these inner events occur in the unconscious mind, which can
be a source of inner strength and healing and can be made
accessible through dreams and psychotherapy. Jung also
argued that changing dangerous and oppressive social conditions depends on the ability of each of us as individuals to
recognize and become responsible for the dark side of our
psyches (the "shadow"), where our capacity for destructiveness originates.

Jung was one of many powerful men who had problems
with his own sexual shadow, and there is evidence that he had

sexual relationships with two female patients. In view of these ethical violations, it is ironic that Jung's work provides a hopeful psychological framework for constructive reconciliation between oppositional viewpoints, whether based on politics, culture, or gender. For instance, it is fundamental to his psychology that men can learn to empathize with and respect women by drawing on innate feminine aspects of themselves ("anima"). Likewise, women can understand and develop capacities they attribute to men by drawing on masculine parts of themselves ("animus"). Although Jung's terminology does not appear in this book, the concepts and approaches I present are decidedly Jungian in orientation.

Jung's violation of the forbidden zone stands as a wound to us all. I can only hope this book in some measure redeems the wrongs committed by him and by many of our cultural fathers.

My hope is that this exploration of sex in the forbidden zone can help men and women become more keenly aware of the differences between life-giving and destructive expressions of sexuality in themselves and in the people around them. With this awareness comes increased power to know when and how to participate in healthy sex, and when and how to reject unhealthy sex. Ultimately the forbidden zone, in its broadest human terms, is held sacred not by laws but by understanding and respect. It is the task of all of us to face the worst of how we treat one another. Doing so offers us a chance to locate what is best in ourselves and, when intimacy calls, to offer no less than our best to the other.

Relationships of Immeasurable Value: The Psychological Heart of the Forbidden Zone

Could I once again get sexually involved with a member of my congregation? Absolutely, if I'm honest about it. I don't want to stop being sexually attracted to what is forbidden. To deny that would be to deny part of my manhood. I understand the need for a boundary, but there is an incomparable excitement in the possibility of going across it. I don't know why it's so important, but it is. To give it up would be like dying.

—REVEREND GRANT BENNETT

Our relationship had a heightened feeling that went right to the divine. With Dr. Yount there was the hope that I could open the vulnerability of my deepest, wounded self, and that it was being welcomed and loved. I hoped that he would touch me, touch the part of me that had been so left out and wounded and rejected, and by touching it bring it, and me, back into life.

—HELEN KIFNER

In these impassioned words we begin to glimpse the enormous psychological forces that both men and women experience in forbidden-zone relationships. This inner dimension of power holds the key to the mystery of why even well-functioning, highly competent men and women can cross the line into mutually destructive sexual involvement.

The sentiments expressed by Helen Kifner point us toward the underlying, nonsexual reasons why women so readily enter forbidden-zone sexual relationships and stay in them past the point of abuse. Reverend Bennett's candor about the lure of the forbidden raises the question of why men are drawn so inexorably toward sexual merger with the women they are supposed to protect that they risk their lives, their fortunes, and their sacred honor for a few stolen moments.

It is clear that for both men and women the special conditions of forbidden-zone intimacy offer access to relationships that are felt to have immeasurable value. Under these circumstances the sudden meeting of a man and woman who have previously been strangers contains the potential to heal the wounds of the past and generate hope for a life filled with self-worth and meaningful connection to others.

While the Prologue of this book summarizes the outer, visible dimension of sex in the forbidden zone, this chapter introduces its psychological heart. For no matter how much we learn about political and social inequalities of power between men and women, we will be unable to alter patterns of sexual exploitation unless we take into account the feelings buried in the psyches of all of us that strongly support forbidden expressions of sexuality.

As a psychiatrist with a particular interest in knowing as much as possible about the inner psychological world of people as well as their outer social reality, I am most concerned with weaving together the way these two dimensions—the outer and the inner—continually interact to create the problem of sex in the forbidden zone.

Following the Jungian model, I see the inner world—the world of our thoughts, memories, feelings, dreams, hopes, and fantasies—as being co-equal with the world outside that we can see, touch, and feel. This inner world, moreover, can be seen, explored, tracked, and mapped as well, but through different sorts of senses. The senses that inform us directly about the inner world are intuition, bodily sensations, emotions, and images in dreams and waking fantasies.

The intricacies of the inner world also can be logically organized, explained, and understood. Inner events have different patterns and logic than do outer events, but once we start tracking the inner world according to its own "language," disparate and seemingly unconnected events can become linked in a relationship as clear as the one between rainfall and sprouting plants.

The inner world is an ecosystem in its own right. In order to grow and thrive, each individual psyche needs a balance of love, shelter, respect, connection to other people, separateness from others, security of the familiar, and stimulation by the unknown. To maintain our inner balance, each of us must be able to experience and recover from the inevitable wounds, pain, loss, and deprivation that life brings.

The process of wounding and healing, of loss and regeneration, continues throughout life as we grow and develop both biologically and psychologically. The modeling we receive in childhood from parents and other important adults determines the way each of us reacts to pain and loss.

If our parents were able to deal in a relatively healthy way with their important losses—such as the loss of a loved one through death or separation, a setback in a career, a period of economic hardship—we will have been given a heritage of hope and faith in ourselves and the world when we suffer our own serious injury. We will be able to wait it out, seek help from others as appropriate, go on with our lives to the extent that we can, and, in time, recover.

At the other end of the spectrum, people who received poor

modeling in their childhood will grow up feeling relatively hopeless about their own ability to heal. When faced with a loss, they may get into deeper trouble by blaming themselves for their misfortunes, feel they have to cover over the pain with drugs, or inflict pain on people around them through psychologically or physically destructive behavior. So-called dysfunctional families pass the message of hopelessness from one generation to the next through patterns of isolation, chemical dependency, and abusive behavior toward one another.

No matter what our childhood experience has been like, we all have, to one degree or another, unhealed wounds. As we emerge from childhood into adulthood, we face the prospect of life wounding us anew. But in almost everybody, no matter how wounded, no matter how hopelessly our families dealt with injury, the hope for restoration of what has been lost, or healing what has been injured, somewhere remains alive.

It is here that we return to the immeasurable value of the forbidden zone. Relationships with trusted professionals hold inordinate power over people's lives precisely because they offer as much hope as they do. At best, therapists, pastors, attorneys, mentors, and teachers heal past injuries, restore meaning, offer access to the deepest resources of self, and even save lives.

When we enter this kind of relationship of trust, we gain access to a new model of coping with life's problems—one that promises to help us transcend the limitations on our lives that we learned in our families. We regain the hope that the wounded parts of us that have been left unhealed might, in the words of Helen Kifner, be "touched and brought back into life." Although women are identified as being in a weaker position in forbidden-zone relationships, men, underneath the social level that invests them with power, are drawn equally to the promise of healing past wounds that these relationships offer.

IMMEASURABLE VALUE FOR WOMEN: NEW AND BOUNDLESS POSSIBILITIES

Each woman I interviewed who engaged in forbidden-zone sex described the immeasurable *nonsexual* value she felt that relationship had attained before any sexual behavior took place. All of them felt that they acceded to sex as a way of maintaining a relationship that had come to have extraordinary importance in their lives and seemed to them to open up new and boundless possibilities for the future.

Most of these women, in trying to account for the reasons they participated in sex with a therapist, pastor, or mentor, despite feeling how wrong it was, also cited the strong influence of cultural factors in their upbringing that steered them toward complying with the sexual desires of these powerful men. They felt that the force of this preexisting message encouraging compliance, when combined with their inner need to hold onto the extraordinary promise offered in the relationship, set up a psychological trap they were powerless to resist.

Patricia Elmont, a psychologist from the Midwest now in her fifties, captures this feeling:

I was twenty-two, married, and had two kids when I first went to see Dr. Stuben because of my depression. I had been raised to be a southern belle and to please men sexually. But I was developing a passion for ideas, too. Dr. Stuben was the first man in my life who was willing to talk with me about ideas. I became enormously excited about going to see him. He was carrying a tremendous power for me, but because of the way I was raised, I just didn't know how to be connected to a powerful man except through seduction. When he said he wanted us to have sex in his office, of course I couldn't say no. It would have never occurred to me to say no. I was horribly lonely and depressed, and because of the part of me he was bringing to life, I needed this man more than ever.

Suzanne Carter, now a university professor, echoed this sense of power when she revealed the feelings that drew her into a secret sexual affair with Dr. Decatur, her mentor at a small educational institute. She was twenty-nine, married, and the mother of two small children. He was forty-five, married, and had a teenage son:

When I first met him, my marriage was very shaky. I was ripe for a waking up. Dr. Decatur represented everything I didn't have in my life. He embodied more capacity than I had ever seen in one person. I had a kind of crush on him, but it wasn't particularly sexual. I felt a recognition and acknowledgment from him, as opposed to feeling pigeon-holed, with no way out, in my marriage. The contrast between that closed-in feeling and what I got from Dr. Decatur was stunning.

Helen Kifner, a successful and outgoing woman nearing fifty, has become an attorney specializing in women's-rights lawsuits. But she was a fragile and isolated young woman of twenty-two when she entered therapy with Dr. Harold Yount, who after several months suggested that they spend their midday sessions having a sexual relationship. In conjunction with the information contained in this chapter's opening quotation, Helen told me,

Dr. Yount was so important to me then—the enormity of his importance was really indescribable. I felt as if my relationship with him was the only thing keeping me alive at the time. How could I have said no when he approached me sexually?

Ten years after an affair with her mentor, Ruth Smythlin, a former divinity student, is still deeply depressed. The event destroyed her ministerial career and brought her to the brink of suicide.

Until the moment he began relating sexually to me, Reverend Clifton had been the most important man I had ever met—a wonderful healer, teacher, and mentor, a man of pure spirit. He brought out my deepest, primal self. He met it and he saw it. I had never in my life been so intimate with a person, and I had tremendous adoration, passion, and love for him, although none of it was sexual. Yet all my work with him is now destroyed, because he insisted we have a sexual relationship. He knew it was hurting me, yet he kept at it.

For women, the powerful forces underlying the sexuality of the forbidden zone emerge clearly as feelings of hope—hope that their deepest wounds can be healed and that their true selves can be awakened, recognized, and brought out of hiding into the vitality of everyday life.

Parent-Child Themes: Injury from Childhood and the Promise of the Future

Why do forbidden-zone relationships hold so much inner power and promise? Part of the answer lies in the unique way in which they simultaneously repeat, yet free us from, the bonds of our relationships with our parents. The forbidden zone implicitly offers the women who enter it a parental quality of trust. This kind of trust invites women to share with men who have previously been strangers the intimacies and injuries of their bodies, their spirits, and their emotions. With this trust men in power encourage women to believe that they will help them toward leading meaningful, productive lives.

The parent-child theme of the forbidden zone is accentuated by the fact that women are particularly vulnerable when they seek help from male doctors, therapists, pastors, and lawyers. Feeling injured and needing care, they find a professional relationship that inevitably allows them to re-experience both the caring and injury that emanate from childhood.

But the forbidden zone confronts the injuries from a woman's childhood with hopes for the future, with yearnings and aspirations for life as it might come to be lived, and for the potential of participating as fully as possible in life. People tend to enter into these relationships when it is critically important for them to transmute past limitations or injuries into future healing and accomplishment.

Understanding how the forbidden zone brings together past injury with future hope deepens our understanding of the place of sex in these relationships. From the heritage of the parent-child bond comes the prohibition of sexuality. From the weight of the future comes the duty for the man to protect, at all costs, the woman's sense of hope and the growth of her aliveness. When the obligation of the past is ignored and betrayed by sexual relating in the forbidden zone, one of the most heartbreaking casualties is the destruction of hope itself.

How Sexuality Enters Relationships of Immeasurable Value

Since the true purpose of this special kind of intimate relationship is to provide nonsexual guardianship of a woman's development, why does sexual fantasy and desire so easily enter the picture? The answer is that sexual intercourse is the ultimate symbol of intimate human relationship. The *act* of intercourse can allow us to experience in the most intense way

possible our deepest biological, emotional, and spiritual striv-
ings, and at the same time allow us to share these feelings with
another person. But the *symbol* of sexual intercourse lives in
our psyches independent of the act, as an inner way for us to
understand what it means to be passionately and meaning-
fully involved—with another person, irrespective of sexuality;
with our own bodies and psyches; or with life itself. Sex can
be an act, but it can also be a highly meaningful metaphor.

Because of this, any relationship that moves us deeply,
even if it is clearly nonsexual, can stimulate sexual fantasy.
The erotic energy in our fantasies can also serve as a medium
of expression for our deepest nonsexual aspirations. Sexual
fantasies can hold the clues to what we need in order to feel
most fully alive, in ways that transcend sex itself. Images of
sexual contact with forbidden partners often represent a need
to make inner contact with a part of ourselves depicted by the
forbidden partner's image.

For instance, when a woman has fantasies about a male
lover, his image can stand for her own need to develop qualities of strength, competence, and self-worth that she might
think of as masculine. Likewise, the women in men's sexual
fantasies can represent his attempt to make contact with less-
developed qualities in his own personality that he perceives as
feminine, such as the capacity for nurturing, comforting, and
closeness.

On a psychological level alone, even without the contribution of the outer power dynamics, there is a tremendous potential for people to involve themselves in exploitative sexual
acts because of the confusion between sexual intercourse as
act and sexual intercourse as symbol. This is a dangerous
liability not only in forbidden-zone relationships but in any
situation in which sexual desire reaches out in a forbidden
direction. Yet by understanding that sexual desire and imag-
ery can have inner meaning when not acted upon, we are
offered a different direction in which to bring our sexuality
when the act itself is harmful to ourselves or to another.

It is precisely because forbidden-zone relationships touch us so deeply that sexual fantasy pours into them. Their tremendous life-giving promise can be fulfilled, for both the man and the woman, even when it presents itself through the potentially dangerous medium of erotic fantasy. What matters in the forbidden zone is not keeping sexual thoughts away, but maintaining a boundary against sexual contact so that the unique potential of these relationships can be realized. Harvesting the nonsexual potential of the forbidden zone takes—beside resisting enactment of the sexual fantasy—time, care, and enormous respect for the power inherent in these relationships.

The Feminine Capacity for Inner Containment of Sexuality

For the men in power who seek healing from their forbidden-zone protégées, cultural messages encourage them to believe that relief from inner pain is inextricably interwoven with sexually consummating a relationship. This stands in marked contrast to the ability of women to describe intensely passionate feelings that remain distinct from being sexual. Although at times women need to engage in physical sexuality as powerfully as do men, women have more capacity to contain sexuality completely as inner experience, and to feel passion as a carrier of nonsexual intimacy.

For example, although Ruth Smythlin felt a "tremendous adoration and passion" for her mentor, these erotic feelings did not translate into sexual desire. The specific distinction Ruth made between a desire *for* intimate relationship with a man but *against* sexual contact seems to be one that women can make more readily than men.

When we move on to examine male sexual psychology, we will see how, in the forbidden zone, the woman's wish to maintain relationship with a man who has become important to her makes her particularly vulnerable when he presses for enactment of his sexual fantasies.

IMMEASURABLE VALUE FOR MEN: THE QUEST FOR SEXUAL HEALING

The power of the forbidden zone has as much impact on a man's psyche as it does on a woman's. Underneath his position of authority and seeming strength, the man is drawn equally to reexperiencing past wounds and the wish to enliven the future. The underlying psychological reality for a man in power that leads to sexual exploitation is that he is as likely to be ministering to his own inner wounds as he is to those of the woman he serves.

Reverend Grant Bennett, whose comments about the power of forbidden sex opened this chapter and who is pastor of a congregation in a midwestern city, began an affair with Julia Noonan, a woman to whom he had been providing pastoral counseling. Reverend Bennett was quite frank in acknowledging that he had begun this affair as a way of healing his depression over a recent divorce:

> Sex has always been very potent for me—it's something I still struggle with. Julia came into my life when I was quite depressed. I was on the one hand mourning my marriage but on the other hand free, feeling the total freedom to do whatever I wanted to do. Julia was very sexual, whereas my wife had been very uptight about sex. Here I was discovering that sex could be fun and joyful. I had never felt that before, and I needed it.
>
> It was as if Julia was being my pastor at the time, because of my needs. The roles were pretty clearly reversed.

She was healing me, even though I knew she wasn't someone I wanted as a partner in life. But it was like being out
of school, like a great weight of responsibility was being
lifted from my shoulders.

Clearly, the men who are the healers in forbidden-zone
relationships often have as much a need to be healed through
them as do their protégées. When a man is feeling his wound
and a woman's sexuality becomes available to him through
the protected, secret conditions of the forbidden zone, the
tendency to avail himself of this opportunity can become irresistible.

Dr. Jim Francis, a respected, successful psychiatrist colleague consulted during the research stages of this book, disclosed that he had had an affair with a patient because he felt
unable to resist the magical healing opportunity that he was
sure sexual contact with her would provide. And even though
I had already accepted that most professional men wrestle
with sexual desire toward the women they serve, I was nevertheless stunned to hear Jim's confession, because outwardly
he seemed to be completely in control. The deeply personal
experiences he shared both shocked and moved me:

Until I finally crossed the line, I had struggled mightily to
never let it happen. But once every few years, my work with
a woman patient would take on such an erotic quality that
I became overcome by my desire to have sex with her. I
fought to maintain control, knowing that the stakes were
extremely high. I've built a career and reputation in my
community. I knew that with one misstep, I would betray
a lot of people I care about: my patients, my students, and
my colleagues, not to mention my wife and family.

Whenever I felt I was losing control, I just prayed that
things would calm down before I became totally overwhelmed. I managed to come through these crises several

times without creating a disaster. Each time I would think: "Never again. I'll never come that close to losing control again." But I never went into therapy to deal with this. I can now admit to myself why not: because I really didn't *want* to prevent myself from experiencing the magic of having sex with a patient.

And then the time came when I felt the eroticism starting to build yet again, and I somehow knew that I was going to go ahead with it. Leah was in her early thirties, and her marriage was in a crisis. She said she loved her husband but was afraid he couldn't return the intimacy she wanted. The crisis was magnified because she wanted to have a child, and he kept putting her off about it. I began being flooded by sexual fantasies about Leah and having a child with her. Then one day, as she was about to leave the office after a particularly painful session, she asked me to hug her. Certainly I should not have responded, but I did. There was no sexuality to our embrace at first, but neither of us made any move to leave it. As we held each other, I began to feel the most minuscule hint of an erection. This in itself did not make me feel that I had crossed the line, because I've accepted that men can sometimes feel an erection as part of strong and warm feelings they are experiencing, without anybody else having to know and without it necessarily signaling sexual desire toward that person.

However—and this was the turning point—I suddenly realized that she could feel my erection against her, and that she was doing nothing to move away. It's difficult to explain how momentous it was for me that she was accepting my sexual self. There was something about this acceptance that opened the floodgates between us. I began giving in to the growing intensity of our bond, knowing that she was feeling it too. Our sensitivity to each other just escalated. My face had been against her neck, so I began kissing her there, and my hands, without even moving, began to feel her body underneath them. She responded to the kisses on her neck. The more sexual I became, the more she accepted and responded. But because I had another patient waiting, we had to stop.

I phoned Leah that night. We were both completely overcome by what had happened, and we scheduled an appointment in my office the next day. We had intercourse then and several other times in the next few weeks. But nothing ever lived up to that magical moment of our first embrace. We both began to feel how wrong it was to have become sexual with each other, but we couldn't go back to being doctor and patient. I referred her to a female therapist and finally went into therapy myself. It's been almost ten years since this happened, and I have no idea what became of Leah or what kind of long-term impact this had on her. As for me, I still live with it as a wounding of her, and myself, that I don't think can ever be healed.

When I asked him, ten years later, what he thought he had learned, this is what he told me:

I think about that first moment when our embrace became sexual. For men the importance of having the erect phallus accepted by a woman cannot be underestimated. It has to do with so much more than simply demonstrating the power of the phallus on an instinctual level. At certain times, the acceptance of our sexual selves is like an acceptance of our total selves, and this holds out the promise of a complete healing and cleansing.

In that moment with Leah I felt that everything that had happened to me in the past—all the pain I had caused others or others had caused me—could be accepted and forgiven. The slate could be wiped clean, and I could be granted a sense of wholeness and self-esteem more complete than I had ever felt before. I know this "slate-wiped-clean" business must sound a little religious, like confession or atonement. Maybe it has that quality, but I think we seek it on a purely psychological, emotional level as well. A great deal of what we men struggle for in our sexual behavior is really a quest to heal ourselves and find value in this world.

But I'm still not sure why we think this validation has to come through sexual contact with a woman. I suppose most of us were raised with the idea that women are to some degree there to take care of us emotionally. Having that special moment with Leah made me feel like the slate was wiped clean for only a few days, then it went away. If we try to get it from a woman, we haven't really earned it, and the source of our wholeness is located in someone else, not in ourselves, which still leaves us dependent on women.

From speaking with men about these issues, I found that the allure of forbidden-zone sex described by Jim Francis is shared by most other men in power. Profound needs for healing and self-validation infuse men's sexual fantasy. Although many men who exploit women are in touch with no motivation more complicated than simple sexual desire and opportunism, I believe the search to heal a wounded sense of self is what underlies most destructive sexual behavior in men.

MEN'S ENVY OF FORBIDDEN SEX: AN EXPLANATION OF THEIR SILENCE

I have already described my difficulty in confronting my ambivalent reaction to the sexual misdeeds of my mentor. My feelings of betrayal and condemnation were accompanied by the clear realization that, somewhere down deep, I wished I could have let myself go toward enacting the fantasy of having sex with a patient. Speaking with men in various professions revealed a nearly universal fascination with the fantasy of sex in the forbidden zone.

When so many men share an inner wish, it shapes their private behavior as well as the way they deal with one another in public. As I discovered through my own experiences with my former mentor, a key element in the perpetuation of sexual abuse by professional men is the public silence of their colleagues—silence that, according to author Elie Wiesel, "hurts the victim most." My research into the link between the psychological and social dynamics of sex in the forbidden zone has led me to conclude that (1) public silence by men about their colleagues' sexual misconduct amounts to tacit *approval* of this misconduct, and (2) the silence is based on the widespread envy that is aroused in men when they hear of their colleagues' sexual exploits.

This envy yields practical ramifications that are absolutely fundamental to understanding and altering patterns of sexual exploitation in our society. We can see that the links between male fantasy and the social dynamics of sex in the forbidden zone are greatly interconnected:

- Although the majority of men holding positions of trust behave ethically in the sense that they will never have sexual contact with a woman under their care, they nevertheless hold onto the hope that one day it may actually happen.
- When men hear about a colleague who has had sexual relations with a woman in the forbidden zone, it encourages this hope.
- Men who never engage in forbidden-zone sex participate in it vicariously through the exploits of men who do. In a tribal sense, it is as if men who violate the forbidden zone are the designated surrogates who live out these fantasies for the rest of the men in the tribe.
- Because these men are the surrogates for the rest of us, we secretly do not wish to prevent them from having sexual relationships with the women under their care.

- Because many men can already barely resist the temptation to engage in sex in the forbidden zone, each episode of actual sexual contact generates, like a virus, an infectious atmosphere that lowers the resistance of men who are struggling not to act on their fantasies.
- And because a deep, healthy, and legitimate search for healing lies behind the masculine wish for forbidden sexuality, men will not give up challenging sexual boundaries until they learn other ways to find what they seek.

This psychological picture, which acknowledges that even ethical professional men wish to leave open the possibility that one day they will have a sexual encounter with a woman under their care, helps to account for the deeply rooted male tendency toward silence, inaction, and suppression of information when it comes to revealing other men's sexual-boundary violations. Efforts to create a more ethical atmosphere in the male-dominated professions are consistently undermined by the less visible dynamics of masculine sexual psychology that I outline here.

Asking men in power to prevent their colleagues' sexual exploitation in some way requires them to undermine their own fantasy lives. Until there has been a further evolution of consciousness about the psychological issues at the heart of sex in the forbidden zone, men will remain psychologically incapable of effectively disciplining themselves for sexual-boundary violations. The medical, psychotherapeutic, pastoral, and legal professions have long insisted on policing themselves about ethical matters. At this stage, however, men in these professions need the help that widespread public scrutiny and growing public understanding can bring to this problem.

But for all of us, men and women, professionals and lay people alike, dealing with the darker side of sexual issues is a difficult challenge. Sexuality provokes highly intimate and personal reactions, some of which we would rather not have to face. My own split between envy and condemnation of my mentor is typical of the difficulty we all have with matters erotic, which are ruled in the human psyche not by logic but by contradiction and paradox.

Our rational minds may go in one direction, trying to adapt reality to preexisting models that make us feel safer, more in control, or in conformity with an ideal of who we think we ought to be. But our less rational sides have highly permeable barriers to sexuality. Dreams, fantasies, and feelings well up from a timeless instinctual world with rules of its own, carrying us toward fuller involvement in the erotic. If we deny what is inside, we can remain equally blind to what is going on around us. As we discover the sources within ourselves that can turn us into sexual victim or victimizer, we can begin to grapple with sexual-boundary problems that were formerly unspeakable, such as rape, incest, and child molestation. Sex in the forbidden zone is in many ways their more mainstream, but equally destructive, parallel.

THE MASCULINE MYTH OF THE FEMININE: DEFERENCE, SEXUALITY, AND DESTRUCTIVENESS

Myths are recurrent stories based on our inner feelings, perceptions, and beliefs. In expressing the most deeply held beliefs of a culture, family, or individual, myths often determine the way we interpret the world around us.

Every family carries its own myths. Some are shared with the culture; others are unique to that family. Exposure to family myths begins the day we are born and plays an enormous role in shaping our perceptions. A family creates a mythic identity for each child that can both help and hinder development of a healthy sense of self. For instance, a family in conflict can endow a particular child with the mythic role of being the family healer. The child develops his abilities to empathize with other people's pain, often at the expense of being given permission to ask for recognition of his own emotional injuries. As an adult, someone with this mythic identity may retain a true gift for healing others but will himself remain emotionally starved.

Family myths can also communicate sweeping judgments that dominate a child's view of life in the outside world. If a family tells its child that the outside world is a place that does not tolerate individuality, that child will be more likely to subordinate his own wishes to outer authority. Another family that holds a positive view of individuality is likely to have a child more capable of putting her own stamp on life.

Cultural myths reach beyond the family to express broadly and deeply held attitudes that can affect every member of a society. Of central importance to the problem of sex in the forbidden zone is a cultural myth I identify here as the "masculine myth of the feminine," which explains the inner attitudes that shape the way women are perceived by men and how women see themselves. Familial and cultural messages strongly encourage both men and women to play out the destructive roles created by this view of women, leaving both genders its victims.

The masculine myth of the feminine invites both women and men to participate in exploitative sex. It consists of three key elements—women's deference, women's special powers, and women as dark and destructive—each of which contributes to our understanding of why professional relationships in which men have power over women are so vulnerable to abusive sexuality.

Women's Deference

In masculine mythology, a woman above all should show deference to a man. The ideal woman is available to a man as a sexual partner, a source of emotional comfort, and a helpmate in running a household and raising children. While each of these qualities can be part of a mutually respectful and satisfying relationship between a man and woman, the flaw is in the demand for deference that underlies most social arrangements between men and women. When it comes to any conflict, the prevalent demand of our culture is that the woman defer to the man, whether the issue concerns practical matters, such as where and how to live, or intimate matters, such as when to make love.

Although the demand for deference from a man can be mixed with love and respect for a woman, its very presence as a value internalized by women sets the stage for sexual exploitation. All of the women I interviewed for this book, even those who have achieved professional and social equality with men, were originally drawn into sexual relating in the forbidden zone through a deeply held sense of deference to the wishes of the man.

Women's Special Powers

The second component of the masculine myth of the feminine involves the tremendous healing, nurturing, and sexual powers that men attribute to women. Men have a firm conviction that women hold these powers in order that they can be bestowed upon men. Attributing these abilities to women drives men toward near-desperation in their attempts to get close to or inside the soul or body of a woman, allowing them to ignore whatever violation may be involved. Nearly all men share the ability to idealize, even deify, the radiant, magical power of the feminine. In this way it can at any moment seem to be the sole object of value worth pursuing in life—regardless of the consequences.

The sexual and seductive components of this attributed power can intoxicate men when they begin fantasizing about contact with a woman. When this intoxication strikes, a woman he knows nothing about may suddenly be seen as a repository of great sexual powers, which can then be turned toward affirming his own sexuality. Especially for men who may be experiencing some problems in this area, the imagined feminine power to arouse becomes an irresistibly compelling attraction.

A man may begin by hoping that a woman is brimming over with her own sexual feelings toward him. Then he confuses his hope with certainty. In breaking down the barrier between his fantasy and reality, he replaces her reality with his mythologized version of her. If he is a male professional and she is under his care, he can permit himself to believe that her erotic powers are so strong as to overwhelm his ability to make an ethical decision to refrain from having a sexual relationship with her.

Women as Dark and Destructive

There is another side to the myth of the healing power that women hold for men. When disappointed, a man's view of this power can easily turn into its very opposite: Women become hateful, vengeful, undermining, and destructive creatures. Men can become certain that whatever ill fate, weakness, or pain has befallen them emanated from the dark powers of a woman.

This theme has deep roots in our culture. In the Book of Genesis, Eve carries out the devil's wishes by tempting Adam to eat from the tree of knowledge, leading to their banishment from Eden. This negative view of feminine power is reflected in such events as the Salem witchcraft persecutions and in literature and drama in the figure of the murderous seductress.

As the prototypical myth expressing the human need to taste forbidden fruit, the banishment from Eden can be interpreted in a way that gives women an unequal share of respon-

sibility for the trouble men have with their instinctual appetites. (My own bias is to interpret eating from the tree of
knowledge as an evolutionary event symbolizing our capacity
for knowing ourselves—which then places in each of us the
responsibility for dealing ethically with our instinctual, including sexual, appetites.)

Men who exploit women are capable of shifting rapidly
among any of the components of this myth they choose to
embrace, depending on circumstances. There are times when
it suits a man to remind a woman of how powerless and
deferential she needs to be, such as when she might be about
to break silence about an exploitative relationship. Men often
invoke the positive side of a woman's sexual power as a defense for having sex in the forbidden zone, by claiming they
acted out of their feelings of love aroused by her. But when
men have been injured, or their position threatened by a
woman showing the least bit of refusal to remain deferential,
the view of the woman can suddenly shift to seeing her as dark
and destructive.

A great deal of the trouble men have confronting sexual
misconduct revolves around their failure to recognize how
conveniently they shift among different aspects of their myth
of the feminine. Between their wish that women remain deferential to masculine power, their occasional rage at women for
not supplying them with nurturing on demand, and their fear
and idealization of feminine power, there can be little room
for honest self-examination.

Although women hold equal responsibility with men for
their choices to be sexual in relationships where there is an
equality of power, so many male-female relationships, in and
out of the forbidden zone, are characterized by a marked
power imbalance favoring men. For this reason, women
who behave seductively in forbidden-zone relationships are
blindly playing out the part of the masculine myth that *wants*
them to behave seductively. For instance, Mia offered herself
to me because she had been taught that she had nothing of

value to offer a man other than her sexuality. As is true for so many women in our culture, she was offered a mythologized masculine view of what a woman should be. She had no choice but to accept it, because she was shown no other way. Psychologically victimized as a child through the devaluation of her feminine sense of self, she embarked on a life-course of repeating this original victimization by allowing, even inviting, sexual exploitation.

Women can be taught this mythologized view of femininity either directly by men or by female role-models whose own self-concept has been shaped to reflect the masculine myth of what women should feel and how they ought to behave. In either case, the result is the same: Their self-esteem is dependent on a man's approval, and the path to approval often includes sexual availability.

The masculine myth of the feminine sheds additional light on the reasons why men are not more vigilant about preventing and punishing sexual exploitation, because a corollary of the myth of feminine sexuality is that a sexually victimized woman "really wanted it." This belief has both its street version (which men apply to cases of rape) and its sophisticated psychological version (built around theories that women have a built-in seductive attitude toward men in power, based on a wish to capture the phallic power of their fathers). In either case, men support one another in blaming the victim for her own plight.

In most cases, the belief that women are being seductive when they are raped or otherwise exploited is pure male fantasy. When the woman has in fact been seductive, men need to understand that this seduction is likely to be a product of years of her adaptation to the masculine myth, whose staying power is attributable not only to its pervasive existence in the psyches of men but to its equally pervasive acceptance in the psyches of women. Yet underneath the part of them that has accepted this myth, I have found nearly all women I have worked with as patients or interviewed for this book to be seeking recognition and respect that is completely *free* of their potential value to men as sexual partners. This even applied to women who at one time used their sexuality expressly to improve a grade, gain prestige, or earn a promotion. Upon reflection years later, these women realized that by playing the seductress they had unknowingly cheated themselves.

If men work to understand their participation in the myth outlined here, they will see how following it leads up a blind alley that denies them the healing they seek through relationships with women. On the other hand, it is a task for women to fight as hard as they can, independent of what men do, to reclaim from purely feminine sources a sense of value that will not allow them to collaborate in their own exploitation.

The immeasurable value of forbidden-zone relationships can be reaped only if men and women turn toward their own wounds and away from making unrealistic demands on one another. The next two chapters discuss in detail the wounds in women and in men that lead them into sex in the forbidden zone.

2

The Wounds of Women

When a woman enters a relationship of importance with a powerful man, a wound from the past is touched and reopened. The presence of the wound generates both intense need and reawakened hope. Need and hope play off against each other, one magnifying the other, until the woman is caught in a swirling crosscurrent of feelings stronger than any she may have previously allowed herself to experience.

As the hope for release from the wound grows, she permits herself to feel more fully the dimensions of pain she has been keeping locked up for so long. The more she allows the pain to be felt, the more dependent she is on the hope—embodied in her relationship with the man—that her wounds can be healed.

Diana Tilton, one of the first women interviewed for this book, poignantly expressed this interrelationship of wound and hope when she related her sexual relationship with her psychiatrist. Diana was in her late thirties, living alone, and working as a lab technician in a doctor's office when she told her story:

Ever since I was a teenager, I had walked around with crazy fears that I would be attacked on the street, or that anyone who got close to me would see how sick I was. I just stayed away from people and lived with these fears. I had been to a number of therapists, but either because I was afraid of them or they of me, I never got any help.

When I was twenty-six, I was referred to Dr. Tower. My hopes rose for the first time in many years when I first went to see him. He seemed old enough and very much in command. I immediately attributed to him the ability to help me, and I began seeing him once a week. At our third session, he told me that his wife and children were out of town, and he had extra time to meet me during the evening at his house. I knew perfectly well what he meant by this, but I went anyway, and of course we ended up having sex. We continued our sexual relationship for three years both in and out of his office.

I've done a lot of thinking about why I went along with him. I remember feeling so desperate when I went to him that I figured the only way I was going to get better was by osmosis, by being around a person who seemed healthy and powerful. Dr. Tower was letting me get close to him through our sexual relationship. The way I saw it, I had absolutely nothing to lose. Of course, I was wrong about that.

It took Diana, whose story will continue later in this chapter, many years and the good fortune of finding a different kind of male therapist to discover that she had completely blocked out memories of an incestuous relationship with her father that lasted from the time she was eight until she was sixteen. Her discovery of this underlying wound unlocked the secret of her overwhelming fears, and it explained why she had been so compliant when Dr. Tower offered what amounted to a repeat of her earlier incest experience.

Although sex in the forbidden zone is psychologically analogous to incest, most women who become sexually involved with men in power do not have as overt a wound as Diana's in their backgrounds. Hers is only one extreme of a spectrum of woundedness that makes women vulnerable to sexual-boundary violations.

Women who have no such overt wounds often find it difficult to understand why they have trouble with men who push against their sexual boundaries. They see themselves as strong and competent, and they therefore tend to blame themselves and exonerate the man if any forbidden-zone violation occurs.

Ruth Smythlin represents this end of the spectrum of woundedness. Despite her recognition of the damaging nature of her sexual relationship with Reverend Clifton, she still, years later, finds it difficult to see herself as a victim:

My father was perfectly proper about boundaries when I was a child, so I feel as if I have no excuses when it comes to my complicity with Reverend Clifton. I knew how wrong our sexual relationship was all along. I feel it was very much my fault, because I couldn't honor my own deep feelings of wrongness about relating that way to him.

Ruth's comments demonstrate how critical it is for women, especially those who do not easily identify themselves as victims, to recover an awareness of the underlying wounds that led them into exploitative sexual relationships. I have grouped the patterns of feminine woundedness that put women at risk for sexual-boundary violations into four categories:

1. Overt sexual or psychological invasion in childhood. Once thought to be highly unusual, more and more adult women are recovering memories of childhood sexual molestation. Others are finding that the effects of continual psychological intrusiveness can also be devastating. The danger for these women lies in re-

peating their loss of control over physical and psychological boundaries.

2. Profound childhood aloneness. Instead of being invaded, some women were left so alone in childhood that they become unselective about the quality of intimate attention they receive as adults. The danger for such women is that any attention at all becomes hard to refuse.

3. Exploited compassion. These women were neither invaded nor left alone. They were highly involved in the emotional life of their families but were given the role of healer to the wounds of their parents and siblings. The danger for such women is that they are highly susceptible to engaging in forbidden-zone sexual relationships as a way of taking care of the wound in the man.

4. Devalued outer potential. This wound, dealt to women by the culture as much as by the family, results from a young woman being told that she "belongs" in the home, as the center of family life, and not out in the world. Such women become especially vulnerable to forbidden-zone relationships with male teachers and mentors who hold out the promise of helping them develop their intellectual, artistic, and vocational talents and ask them to pay the price sexually.

PHYSICAL AND PSYCHOLOGICAL BOUNDARY INVASIONS: LOOKING FOR SOMETHING ELSE

Boundary invasions in families range from overtly incestuous sexual assaults to continual psychological incursions. While Diana Tilton's physical relationship with her therapist overtly repeated the incestuous invasion by her father, Barbara Forsch, a psychotherapist in her early forties, experienced no actual sexual molestation as a child but feels that the magnitude of the psychological invasiveness she did experience left her completely confused about her sexual boundaries—so much so that she considered it a triumph when, in her twenties, she was able to seduce her psychiatrist into carrying on a year-long relationship during their therapy sessions. This is how Barbara describes, twenty years later, the wound that led her into forbidden-zone sex:

> I feel as if the invasion started literally the day I was born. As a child, my parents would always criticize and organize my spontaneous playing, telling me some other way I should be doing it. As a teenager my mother began to develop a kind of sexual paranoia about me, as if she had this fantasy that I was having sex, although I was then completely innocent. She kept warning me about what boys might do to me but would never respond when I asked her for real information. She went through my drawers, opened my mail, listened in on phone calls, and checked my underpants when I took them off—anything that had to do with me was for my mother's hands and eyes. I felt parts of my body belonged to other people. Because my boundaries were so messed up, it was almost inevitable that I would not be the one to perceive that I shouldn't have sex with my shrink.

Barbara's experience typifies a multigenerational tragedy in which the vulnerability to boundary invasion is handed down, continually, from mother to daughter. Her mother's failure to respect intimate boundaries bequeathed to Barbara an extreme vulnerability to sexual incursion from any authority figure, male or female. It is becoming clear from research that abusive mothers were often themselves physically or sexually abused as children, and are blindly handing down this dark legacy to their children.

Yet even women whose early lives have been marked by

abuse are able to carry hopeful, restorative fantasies into future helping relationships. As adults, these women often seek out male authority figures, hoping for a different, nonabusive outcome. But in their confusion about setting boundaries, women who have been physically or psychologically invaded as children are the least able to defend the forbidden-zone barrier when a man begins to invade it. And so their fragile hopeful fantasies are killed off once and for all by yet another sexual incursion.

Women who have such unformed boundaries are at great risk to offer themselves sexually to men. Emotionally, they are unable to distinguish between relationships in which sex belongs and those in which it does not. As Barbara put it:

I went to my third session with Dr. Adams with my raincoat on and nothing but underwear underneath. When it was time to go I took off my coat and rubbed up against him. He was kind of passive about it, but I could tell that he was going to let it keep happening. It just escalated from there. But now I see that everything that pushed me to be sexual with him was with me before I ever walked into his office. He looked real good to me by contrast with my family. I could see he was attracted to me, and I wanted to make myself important to him.

I was always looking for something else, and he was part of that something else. He could have been a gift, a positive gift. He could have said he wasn't going to have sex with me. He could have said, "I see what you're doing, and I totally understand, but I can't do this with you. Let's talk about what goes on inside you that you have to do this." He didn't need to sexualize the therapy, even if I did. I could have started recovering then. Instead, I felt more crippled than ever. It's taken me years to stop hating myself for what happened with that doctor.

I'm still trying to escape feeling punished every day for

the sick sexual relationships I have been in. I've had a lot of therapy in the ten years since I stopped seeing Dr. Adams, but every experience seems to bring it back. I'm living with a man now, and trying to learn how to be intimate again in a healthier way. But whenever we get particularly close, something in me just pulls away and says, *This is gross, this is out of the question.* I don't know if I'll ever get over that feeling when I get close to a man.

PROFOUND ALONENESS: THE UNRECOGNIZED INNER SELF

Women who have been left alone rather than invaded can bring just as profound a wound to the forbidden zone. They have been deprived of companionship and validation in ways that make them equally vulnerable to invasion. No matter how many people appear to populate their lives, inside they feel so alone that they will allow their bodies to be touched whenever there is any semblance of warmth or caring. Because helping relationships presume some level of care, the woman who is inwardly so alone will allow virtually any man in a position of trust to touch her sexually.

It is important to distinguish between this kind of sad aloneness and a different quality of aloneness that some women feel, within which they are able to experience a somewhat positive sense of self. Such women may be socially isolated, but inside they are sustained by a strong feeling of their own identity and self-worth. Because they define themselves through highly individualized values rather than by cultural standards, these women, although isolated and alone, may be at the lowest risk for sexual-boundary violations. Although they may suffer in their aloneness, they accept very little of the cultural stereotyping that encourages women to tolerate, if not collaborate with, men who push against the sexual boundary.

The women whose aloneness puts them at risk for boundary violation lack a central source of self-esteem, which fails to develop when a parent or parent figure has not truly recognized and valued their inner core. This failure often occurs when parents are themselves so injured that they become unable to respond to the needs of their children. Because it goes unrecognized by her parents, the child loses contact with her inner aliveness.

She also may adapt herself to trying to heal her parents' injuries. This is a recognizable pattern many adults are working on in addiction groups and adult-children-of-alcoholics groups. This kind of parenting can create a split between a well-adapted visible outer personality and an injured, alone inner self. Such splits occur when parents and society place too high a premium on children conforming to standards of outer behavior, at the expense of validating the child's inner feelings, choices, and aspirations.

The child in this situation usually grows up with a good deal of hatred toward the rejected, but more authentic, inner self. Ruth Smythlin, who had had a long, secret affair with the married dean of her divinity school, related that in her ostensibly stable family her parents used to say, out of the blue, "You sure are a wonderful person." She explained further:

You would think that would make me feel very good, but the problem was that they never said it in relation to anything I thought or said or did, unless I just happened to have done something that fit into their plan for me. This is the only way I would ever get approval from them. In fact, my experience was that when I expressed *myself*, whatever I said or did was ignored, discounted, punished, or ridiculed.

I now see how this undermined my deep intuition about both myself and other people. It had a great deal to do with why I couldn't trust my instinct to say no when Reverend Clifton approached me sexually. After all, I knew perfectly well what kind of outer behavior would meet with *his* approval.

Many forbidden-zone relationships fatally reenact such scenarios: a woman, closed down to herself but adapted to meet the expectations of others, puts hope and trust in a male therapist, teacher, pastor, or lawyer. When he attempts to sexualize their relationship, the woman, by deep inner training, is preadapted to numbly turn over her body and sexuality to his needs.

The close relationship between the profound aloneness that comes from lack of recognition in childhood and the inability to create sexual boundaries later in life is addressed in Sue Miller's novel *The Good Mother.* The state of mind that results is well depicted by protagonist Anna Dunlap, who loses custody of her daughter because of an alleged sexual indiscretion committed by her boyfriend. Anna's wounded sense of self, which eventually prevents her from fighting harder for her daughter in the custody battle, is recounted through her own memories of an emotionally barren childhood and an adolescence in which she allowed herself to become a sexual victim. Anna recalls how she had little sense of self at high school parties:

I did nothing while a whole series of boys ground groaning against me, their eyes shut against seeing me, their hands on my breasts, and finally in my blouse, up my skirt. I felt nothing, less than nothing.

Anna describes her recognition that it was her responsibility to create a sexual boundary at the same time as she realizes that she was powerless to do so:

His hand moved in on my breast, cupped it. He seemed
to wait a moment for me to protest, and then his hand
began a possessive massage. I was frozen. If I didn't want
this, I had to say no. I had to say *no* out loud. I had to
acknowledge what he was doing, and tell him to stop, or
move his hand, or laugh and slap him as I had heard
several other girls do around the room. I did nothing.
. . . I knew from what the other girls said that they felt
. . . *in charge* of it all . . . whereas I didn't know what to
do, and so did nothing.

Anna goes on to experience the self-hating consequences of
her inability to guard her boundaries:

Now there was nowhere in my life I felt at home. I felt
completely false to myself, that there wasn't any center
to me, that there was no situation in which I told the
truth or acted on the truth with anyone. . . . After one
party where two different boys had pushed me into the
darkest corner of the room to rub up against me, I swal-
lowed twelve aspirin. I held lighted matches to the skin
of my forearm. Nothing was sufficient to restore to me
my forgotten sense of self.

It is the "forgotten sense of self" that leaves women unable
to find the voice to say no when they are sexually invaded. This
is precisely the wound that renders many women unable to
defy a man who wishes to exploit the trust of the forbidden
zone through sexual contact.

EXPLOITED COMPASSION:
HEALING MEN SEXUALLY

When children are treated as extensions of the needs of their
emotionally injured parents, they are so used to being exploited that it becomes a way of life. Because children are

vulnerable and close to their own injuries, they can be highly attuned to their parents' emotional states. They have a natural capacity for developing compassion for their parents' injuries. Parents can exploit this by allowing their children to assume the role of healer.

Girls whose compassion has been exploited in the service of their parents' wounds are at high risk as adults to repeat that behavior with men. Hidden in the forbidden-zone sexual demands of even the most powerful men are underlying wounds that cry out for sexual healing. Women have been encouraged to respond directly to these wounds. Sex, in and out of the forbidden zone, can become the adult medium through which a woman continues to play out the childhood scenario of healing those around her.

Helen Kifner, the attorney who as a young woman could not turn away her therapist's sexual advances, is now able to see his wound:

Of course, what allowed him to assume so much impor-tance to me was that I felt like the wounded, rejected little girl he was willing to accept. But now I see how wounded he was, how he drew me closer to him not for me, but for himself. If I really think back to that time, I knew and felt this all the while, that I was ministering to his wounds. But I wasn't able to let myself feel too much of his underlying weakness, partially because I was unwittingly participating in the cultural myth of "powerful father bestows strength on needy, weakened daughter."

I have to admit to a deeper reason, which is that I *needed* his strength at that point, so I tried very hard to continue to see it in him. What got me out of the relationship was that as time went on I was able to see more of his weakness and feel how he was sapping my strength. At this point I began to get angry—and instead of having compassion for his weakness, I saw in it a seedy, dirty-old-man quality that made me sick.

When a woman who has been sexually exploited acknowledges her role as the compassionate sexual healer to men, she
begins to stop colluding in the central dynamic of being bound
to a man who is exploiting her. In beginning to value her
capacity for compassion while understanding that she has
expressed it in destructive ways, she gains the ability to break
free of the exploitative pattern.

But some men, such as Diana Tilton's Dr. Tower (who after
three sessions mentioned that his wife and children were out
of town and suggested they meet during the evening at his
house), will go to great lengths to deny that the women they
are exploiting have any healing value to them. As their sexual
relationship developed, Dr. Tower became verbally abusive to
Diana, degrading her and forcing her to play the role of the
helpless patient. By making her feel even more helpless and
degraded, he assured himself that she would be unable to
leave him:

> Although I was so needy that my life began to revolve
> around him, the sex itself was just a disaster. He became
> very degrading to me, saying that he could be having sex
> with any number of women who would satisfy him more
> than I would, and that this was a waste of his time. I told
> him I would be happy to stop our sexual relationship, be-
> cause by now I saw that this was not the answer to my
> problems. But the curious thing was that he didn't want it
> to stop. He insisted we keep having sex, even though he
> continued telling me how awful it was.

Such misalliances are extremely frequent between men
and women. In these relationships a woman's compassion,
which emanates from her most intimate wish for human connection, has been used as a commodity. As the relationship,
flawed from the start, continues to deteriorate, the woman
becomes increasingly self-critical, faulting her ability to love.

As long as this loving quality is exploited rather than respected, the true inner self that yearns for connection and acceptance recedes farther and farther from life. Pushed far enough away, the true self can become irretrievable.

Diana's observation that "the sex itself was a disaster" reflects a nearly universal reaction among the women I interviewed. Not one of them used the term "make love" in describing their sexual activities in the forbidden zone. Relayed was a marked lack of tenderness and consideration for the women on the part of the men, which clearly reflected the underlying exploitative psychological reality. The sexual acts themselves engendered in the women no physical pleasure; instead they caused actual pain, nausea, or feelings of numbness and deadness.

It would seem that the deep human wrong being committed by sex in the forbidden zone prevents even the sort of excitement that impersonal sex sometimes offers. When the relationship is so fundamentally flawed, the inner self recognizes this and permits the body little or no pleasure.

DEVALUED OUTER POTENTIAL: FEMININITY TURNED AGAINST ITSELF

Women bring another level of injury to the forbidden zone, one that is less visible than the wounds just described because it is manifested in our society's most competent and ostensibly healthy women. This injury emanates from the culture and is delivered at home, in schools, and in the media. It is the wound of femininity turned against itself—a damaging judgment that communicates to them that what they have to offer the world outside the home is less valuable than what men have to offer, and that the particularly feminine values they carry are a liability in the workplace, the political arena, and in public life.

As a result, women feel that their lives are closed in, restricted, and impaired. When a woman meets a man—as mentor, healer, protector—who has the connection to the world at large that she yearns for, all that she might become is for a moment in his hands.

Despite signs of gradual change, the gender-related division of labor in society still encourages men to develop themselves in visible ways in the world, while pushing women to develop themselves invisibly. Women can devote their lives to the artful and difficult tasks of nurturing men's feelings, homes, and families without any of their work being acknowledged in the outside world.

When a woman wants her work to cross over into the world of the socially visible, she almost always encounters men as the guardians of this crossing. If, from childhood onward, her outer-world aspirations have been treated with respect and equality by her parents, and especially by her father and male teachers, the outer world will appear to be relatively accessible to her. Men will still guard the crossing, but she will have learned that there is room for her in their world.

The wounds that block off her outer potential come when her outer-world aspirations are ignored, ridiculed, and patronized. These barriers can become psychologically insurmountable when a man purports to usher her into the outside world as his protégée but demands a price for it—a price that can be exacted through her spirit or through her body.

Dr. Marian Cravath, a prominent child psychologist, paid the price with her body for her mentorship. She was one of the many professional women I sought out for an expert viewpoint on treating victims of sexual exploitation who instead proffered her own relevant experiences.

When Marian was a graduate student in psychology, the mentor who had inspired her professional career made it clear that he wanted to sleep with her, despite the fact that both of them were married.

Dr. Martin had changed my life. I came from a family that in no way validated my inner voice, my sense of myself, my interest in ideas and the outside world. I was left shut down and very depressed. I didn't even know that I had a mind until I met him. All my parents wanted of me was to be attractive to men and get them some grandchildren, and I had gone right to work accomplishing that.

But everything changed when I got to college and took a course with Dr. Martin. He was a tremendously inspiring teacher. I gobbled up everything he said. I loved talking to him about ideas, and I began studying psychology with great passion and energy. It was wonderful for me. As I began to get some personal recognition from him, his importance in my life just grew. If Dr. Martin mentioned Béla Bartók, you could be damn well sure I was at the library the very next day finding out who Béla Bartók was and whether I was saying it right.

Despite her lack of sexual interest toward him and the fact that marital fidelity was a central value of hers, she found herself unaccountably ready to accede when one day, in his office, he simply embraced her and started kissing her. Dr. Martin had been the catalyst of her entire academic career, of her belief in her own capacity. He had recognized her talent and brought her back to a life of the mind, freeing her from the limitations her family had imposed. When she was on the verge of becoming a psychologist in her own right, Martin, as Marian put it, "decided to cash in his chips with me."

Feeling unable to refuse him for fear of rupturing their relationship, she submitted, meeting him to have sex several afternoons a week in motels. After six months, he told her that he had become involved in a liaison with another student and broke off not only their affair but their teacher-student relationship.

Marian immediately went into a deep depression. She was unable to complete her degree in psychology, and when her husband learned of the affair, her marriage broke up. But the long-term effect was even more devastating, because the sexual violation went straight to the heart of Marian's wound, her blocked-off potential. Until it became sexual, their relationship had been healing that wound, releasing Marian to use her intellectual capacity in a visible way, instead of forcing her to play the more culturally sanctioned role of "wife": sexual partner, mother, keeper of the home, keeper of the feelings.

Once faced with the fact that Martin, finally, exacted the precise demand for sexual availability that she had felt he was releasing her from, Marian's inner world was shattered. Robbed of the hope that her intellect and vigor could be expressed in their own right, she shut herself off from life.

For the next year I sat around my house in a deep depression, staying in front of the furnace trying to keep warm. I was constantly preoccupied with alternating feelings of hating Dr. Martin, feeling abused, ripped off, guilty, and then missing him dreadfully and longing for the relationship we had before it became sexual, when he had been so respectful, so enabling to me.

I spent a number of years trying to heal my own wound by actually getting deeper into it: being seductive and sexual with men, trying to be beautiful and interesting and dynamic with them. And I was good at it. How wonderful it could have been, and this still makes me so sad, if he could have understood and respected how exciting and exhilarating it was for me to learn from him and have him as a mentor. But instead he led me totally away from myself. I came close to never getting it back.

There can be injury to a woman even if she resists a man's incursion into the forbidden zone: He makes it impossible for her to continue their relationship, so she loses a teacher, a healer, a guide. Any such loss may be the critical one that dooms a woman to years or a lifetime of hopelessness about fulfilling her aliveness in relationship or in work.

THE DAMAGE OF SEXUAL BETRAYAL: SIMILARITIES TO RAPE AND INCEST

Women bring wounds of childhood to adult relationships of trust with men, looking, in Barbara Forsch's words, "for something else." When these relationships are sexually betrayed, the magnitude of damage must be understood in terms of the similarities to rape and incest.

Rape is the commission of sexual intercourse forcibly and without consent. The law has come to recognize that unless a person is psychologically free to say *either* yes or no, consent cannot be given even if at the time of the sex act the person says yes. Although none of the women I interviewed were forcibly raped, all of them admitted feeling a lack of freedom of consent in the sexual relationships they had with men in the forbidden zone. As Ruth Smythlin said, "I couldn't honor my own very deep feelings about sexual misconduct when he approached me, so I went ahead even though it nauseated me."

Women go against their deep feelings in this way because force is being applied to them emotionally, if not physically. The emotional currents in human relationships can apply the strongest forces imaginable, especially if the relationship has a parent-child quality to it. Without any physical basis, children sometimes feel that they will die if they make their parents unhappy with them. If children feel unloved and abandoned, they will do anything to win back the love of their parents, accepting them on any terms, no matter how much abuse they have suffered.

Because the forbidden zone reawakens these childlike parts within us, acquiescence to sex under these emotional circumstances can hardly be equated with adult consent. In the light of these underlying dynamics, there can be no such thing as consent, in the adult sense, to a sexual act by a woman with a man who has power over her in the forbidden zone. A man in this position of trust and authority becomes unavoidably a parent figure and is charged with the ethical responsibilities of the parenting role. Violations of these boundaries are, psychologically speaking, not only rapes but also acts of incest.

There is a pattern of symptoms that rape victims experience called "rape trauma syndrome," characterized by overwhelming feelings of depression, fear, anxiety, guilt, and shame. There is usually an absence of anger, an emotion that helps a victim recover from the trauma of sexual assault, because she is too afraid to become angry. Incest victims display many of the same symptoms. My research in this field suggests that a similar response pattern applies to victims of sexual exploitation in the forbidden zone.

Women who have had sex in the forbidden zone also share with rape and incest victims the tendency to blame themselves for the acts of forbidden sexuality in which they have participated. In this respect they collaborate with the viewpoint of their male victimizers who try to evade responsibility by blaming their victims. This is yet another element of the self-defeating vicious circle that heaps abuse on top of abuse.

Because of their own guilt and fear, victims tend not to report sexual assault, whether it is incest, rape, or erotic contact with a man in a professional relationship. Women who report any of these violations are often subjected to further humiliation and brutalization as they try to enlist the aid of authorities in bringing their victimizers to justice. Thus the cycle continues.

A Death of Hope: The Effect of Forbidden-Zone Sex on the Maternal Instinct

A surprising effect in these women has been a previously unreported kind of damage—the failure to bear children after the forbidden-zone sexual experience. Conceiving a child is often a symbol of hope, and becoming a parent can be both an opportunity for reworking injuries from one's own parents and a fulfillment of one's own potential. I found it both striking and sad that although all the women interviewed for this book have spent years trying to find their way back to recovery from their injuries, not one of them has yet borne a child since her experience of sex in the forbidden zone.

Some of the women were already mothers when they had their forbidden-zone sexual experience. The pain, turmoil, and injury to their marriages strongly interfered with the aspirations they might have had to bear another child.

Others, still childless in their twenties when they became sexually entangled, have spent years feeling profoundly damaged because of this sexual violation, and only two of them have, quite recently, even attempted a marital-quality relationship. All of them now feel the pressure of the future upon them, the "biological clock." They either know or fear that the time needed to heal this damage sufficiently to conceive a child may take longer than the span of biological fertility still left to them.

Diana Tilton put it this way:

> To say that I would want a child would be to say that I'm healthy enough for it. But I'm not yet. I would have to do a lot of transforming in order for that to happen, and there just won't be time. It's a loss I don't have any control over.

And Ruth Smythlin links her ambivalence about having a child directly to her forbidden-zone sexual experience:

I'm not sure whether I want to have a child. I have mixed feelings. When I talk about what happened with Reverend Clifton, my self-doubt and shame are so strong that I don't think I could be a parent.

Childbearing is by no means the only way of regaining hope and a sense of self. Some of the women interviewed have begun to recover a sense of their future; others are still struggling for it and may find their way to a psychological and spiritual fertility not dependent on biology.

As a symbol, however, the lack of childbearing after the injury of forbidden-zone sex suggests that the damage it creates goes to the very core of feminine existence, in much the same way as do the wounds of rape and incest.

3

The Wounds of Men

Masculine woundedness is an elusive but absolutely crucial ingredient in the fatal conspiracy between men and women that leads to exploitative sex. The wounds of men remain hidden behind a vast cloud of masculine erotic fantasy and folklore that organizes itself around the masculine myth of women, including their sexual availability. Because all men are in some way wounded, and because their quest for healing usually takes the form of seeking sexual contact, an understanding of their wounds can form a basis for men to discover nonexploitative ways to heal themselves.

But as long as a man believes he has a right to make sexual contact with a woman who is forbidden to him—be she patient, employee, or student—he can put off facing his own wound, examining his own motivation, and therefore stopping his exploitative act. And as long as cultural values implicitly forgive—even admire—those who engage in sexual misconduct, men will have little incentive to focus on their own wounds, concentrating their attention instead on how to cross over the next forbidden boundary.

So for the man who wishes to change, and for the woman who wants to understand men, here is a chance to explore the link between masculine psychological woundedness and the forces that lead men to exploit women sexually. As with women and their wounds, men experience their injuries through a variety of symptoms—feelings of depression, self-hatred, inadequacy, and a sense of meaninglessness. They also experience a loss of the ability to perceive how they hurt others, loss of control leading to violent or addictive behavior, and ultimately loss of family, friends, and livelihood.

Certainly a man who is depressed and feeling a lack of meaning in his life is at greater risk to exploit a woman over whom he has power than is a man who is content with his life. But the sorts of wounds I present are not categorized in terms of the immediate feelings men have at the moments they exploit women; they are framed instead as the source of longer-term, underlying psychological patterns that make men particularly vulnerable to the immediacy of sexual energy as it presents itself in forbidden-zone relationships. They are grouped as follows: wounds from the culture, wounds from the father, and wounds from the mother.

WOUNDS FROM THE CULTURE

The Devaluation of Sexual Fantasy and the Inner World

The importance to men of sexual fantasy about women cannot be underestimated. Sexual fantasy is such a central element in the psychological life of men that it often captures a man's interest more than the woman he is with. More important, fantasy is the inner theatre in which a man attempts to make contact with all the magical and dangerous possibilities that the feminine world holds for him. The world of sexual fantasy actually provides a man with an unparalleled psychological opportunity: Vast resources of life-enhancing vitality are suddenly made available as he feels erotic interest in the woman who is forbidden to him.

Every act of sexual exploitation between a man and a woman has been shaped and nourished by countless hours of masculine sexual fantasy. When not used as a pretext for exploitation, man's captivation by sexual fantasy in itself represents a completely healthy and natural way to explore the world of the feminine. But this attempt to learn about qualities that a man sees as feminine has become twisted by the cultural and familial messages men receive, which both devalues sexual fantasy as inner experience and encourages men to enact the fantasy with a flesh-and-blood woman instead.

When we enter the realm of our sexual fantasies, we are able to make contact with levels of inner reality that our culture has hidden from us. A man's fantasies of women are in large part inner images of his own self that he can experience in no other way because those elements have been rejected as "feminine." These qualities include receptivity, vulnerability, inner-directedness, nurturing, and noncompetitiveness.

Submerging the Wound

Our culture encourages men to submerge and ignore the wounded, vulnerable element of their psyches. The same cultural bargain that endows men with strength in the outer, social realm paradoxically weakens them in the inner, psychological dimension. Men are taught to deny illness and weakness, whereas women are encouraged to identify with the role of the weak, vulnerable, or sick person. This social mythology discourages women from expressing their strength, and in denying masculine woundedness and pain takes from men their ability to be healed. For it is a prerequisite of psychological healing that pain first be acknowledged.

When psychological wounds are denied, they constantly press for our attention by creating symptoms: anxieties, depression, obsessions, destructive behavior. And for men, the fantasy of sexual merger with a woman almost universally presents itself as a way to assuage their wounds.

Dr. William Rin, a clinical psychologist, describes the way his own underlying wound led to a sexual encounter with a patient:

I was in my mid-forties then, and to the outside world I had everything: a good marriage, healthy children, a prominent teaching position at the university, and a thriving private practice. But underneath it all I was completely depressed, although I never told this to anyone. I was just so scared to appear weak, and all these people were counting on me, so beginning in my mid-thirties, when I should have gotten some help, I just got into a vicious cycle of depression, hiding it, more depression, and isolation from my true feelings.

For a while, I was too depressed even to have sexual fantasies. But I started noticing that I began having them about more and more of my women patients. I knew I was beginning to feed off them emotionally, but these fantasies were my only source of pleasure, so I still didn't go get the help I obviously needed.

Then I began seeing a new patient, Linda Hull. She had a vulnerable quality that probably allowed me to see my depressed self in her, although I didn't know that at the time. From the first day she walked into my office, I began being flooded by fantasies that she and I would become intimate. I did nothing to fight off these fantasies. Instead, I just started manipulating the situation so that I could draw her into a sexual relationship. Even though I knew how wrong it would be, I didn't want to stop myself from going ahead. One day I couldn't wait any longer, and I just walked over to her chair when she was crying and started kissing and caressing her. She offered no resistance, and we had intercourse. For a few brief seconds, I felt my fantasy was being fulfilled. I was suddenly, magically being brought back to life. Then I saw

what I had done to Linda and how I had deluded myself,
and it all went away.

I had wanted her, and I took her. I wasn't thinking at all
about what it might mean to her. She never brought charges
against me; she just left my office and never returned. But
I know I seriously harmed her. I wish it weren't part of my
past.

Dr. Rin's self-reproach and continuing feelings of emptiness also illustrate the blind alley men find themselves in
when they act out exploitative scenarios with women. They
can have the sexual contact if they insist; but it takes them
farther and farther away from the healing they seek.

The depression Dr. Rin describes seems to be an occupa-
tional hazard of men in power. It is well known, for instance,
that male doctors and therapists are at far greater risk for
suicide than are members of the general population. They and
all men in leadership positions often hide chronic depression
for years behind a show of strength. In addition to this, a man
may have additional concerns: divorce, a failed love affair,
loss of professional prestige, and mid-life adjustment to growing old, which add to his psychological distress.

These feelings of vulnerability and fear do not fit the ap-
proved masculine cultural image. Beginning in childhood,
when boys find themselves facing loss, they are encouraged to
suppress the feelings inside, ignore them, or simply stop having them. They are often told that having feelings, especially
painful ones, is a feminine trait.

Eventually, men who have trouble putting aside their
feelings are likely to be labeled weak and oversensitive, and
they begin to hate themselves for feeling so much. The men
who successfully hide such feelings within are better
equipped to become publicly acknowledged leaders and
heroes. Yet there is a heavy price for this kind of masculine

success: It comes at the expense of a man victimizing parts of himself, and it lays the groundwork for him to victimize others.

The Reappearance of the Wounded Feminine

It is not so easy to kill off parts of ourselves, no matter how strongly we are encouraged to do so. There are serious consequences for men who submerge their wounds. What happens to the "feminine" feelings that are stuffed away, ignored, and no longer felt? Remaining very much alive, they reappear to men as motifs in their sexual fantasies.

The psyche is quite clever. If it has been told that whole categories of feelings are feminine, it creates an image of a woman to embody these feelings. Men carry these feminine images, representing their own split-off feelings, with them at all times. Then when a man enters a relationship of trust with a woman, this inner feminine image gains a flesh-and-blood counterpart, right there in the room with him.

Imagine a man in this position—a doctor, lawyer, pastor, professor, or businessman—who has never been able to acknowledge his so-called feminine feelings. Indeed, he has been taught to be quite afraid of them. He looks across the room to the woman with whom he has developed some professional intimacy. The reality of who she is becomes indistinguishable from the inner image of a woman that he carries with him. As fantasy and reality overlap, the man begins to project into her body and spirit the "feminine" feeling potential and mystery that he has shut himself off from. He will be drawn to her for healing, for contact with what he hopes will be an unexpected new source of aliveness.

When a man in a position of power meets with a protégée behind closed doors, the world of sexual fantasy is invited in as an honored guest. The mutual participation of a man and a woman in this fantasy world is a central dynamic of forbidden-zone relationships of every kind.

It is important for a woman in therapy to be able to allow herself to express her dream and fantasy life freely, so that all parts of her psychological being become available to the healing process. But the male therapist can be drawn beyond listening toward actual psychological participation with his patient's life. Her fantasies, hopes, and dreams may touch him, infuriate him, puzzle him, fascinate him, and stimulate his own fantasy life.

This process is readily identifiable in therapy, but it is also present in all of the professions subject to forbidden-zone conditions of trust. Men in power fantasize about the women under their care at least as much as these women fantasize about them. A man's fantasy-image is his own. The real woman is not. He has the right to imagine communion, intimacy, and sexual contact of the most intense kind possible with his inner image. But sex in the forbidden zone becomes a reality when a man feels, as he often does, that he has the right to touch the woman who is actually with him in the room.

The Quest for Intimacy in Sexual Fantasy

The intense quest for the enlivening powers of intimacy with the feminine helps explain why fantasies of forbidden women have special power. In their fantasies, most men create images of sexual intimacies far beyond the levels of intimacy they are likely to have experienced in their actual relationships with women. The richness of this inner experience helps explain why the world of masculine sexual fantasy is so well guarded against intrusions from the real world that might dilute its power.

Men allow themselves a miasma of feeling states through these fantasies that they rarely allow elsewhere. Positive states

such as trust, exploration, nourishment, softness, love, gener-
osity, freedom from demand and from constraints of time—
all of these can be summoned through erotic images of intimate contact, without shame. And they can take place
between any part of the man's body and any part of the
woman's body. The psyche uses these images of physical contact as a metaphor for the deepest possible emotional and
spiritual connections.

Other feeling states that often come up in masculine sexual
fantasy involve the man's hidden capacity to give or receive
the unselfish, nurturing care that is usually considered to be
a feminine trait. Because men in our culture are discouraged
from expressing these qualities, it is usually only in their
dreams and sexual fantasies that they can rediscover them.

Feeling Like a Woman: The Demeaned Feminine

Of course, fantasies can also become an arena for negative
feeling states. Helplessness, anger, attack, intrusion, dismem-
berment, even murderous feelings can be discharged and experienced. Such negative states, in which sadistic, aggressive,
and murderous fantasies can be mixed with loving and plea-
surable ones, represent another hidden level of experience
available to men through sexual fantasy. It is through these
images that a man can also make contact with the demeaned
feminine aspect of our culture.

The seeds of a man's ability to develop compassion for the
suffering feminine lie in his own fantasy life. When his fantasies place him on the receiving end of humiliation and degra-
dation, he can share in the feminine experience of what it feels
like to be sexually abused and victimized. This can help a man
put restraints on his own exploitative behavior.

Many men find, in their quest for experiencing the feminine, that sexual fantasies and dreams bring them as close as
they will ever get to feeling what it is like to be a woman. This
experience can take different forms. Men frequently have

images of being entered or penetrated, of wearing women's clothing, or of discovering that they have female genitalia.

One can interpret these images as merely expressing a man's fear of losing his phallic power, but that overlooks an important point. Such dreams and fantasies can instead be seen as a quest by a man to move toward knowing something about what it is like to be feminine, or at least to provide some basis of masculine empathy with the feminine experience. This empathy, brought to bear by a man at a moment that might otherwise lead him into a sexually exploitative act, could allow him instead to honor his protégée's trust, and his own self as well, with the restraint that can come only from empathy for someone else's suffering.

But it is just at this point that a man can make a terrible mistake: He may fail to understand that the woman in his sexual fantasy, no matter how strongly she resembles an actual woman, is really an embodiment of life-giving feelings that have been lost to him through his adaptation to "maleness" in society. When men can come to see their fantasy lives as the worship of their own inner images of the feminine, they can gain access on their own to the life-affirming qualities they believe are obtainable only through contact with the female body.

When my male patients report dreams or compelling fantasies of sexual contact with a woman, I may ask them to try seeing the woman's image as a representation of an inner quality of their own. Many of them are startled but also deeply relieved to hear that there is another way to understand and deal with their inner sexual theatre besides replaying their quest for contact with a woman. Looking at their sexual fantasizing as a search for realization of their own inner qualities gives them a new kind of self-respect and respect for women.

But the wound from the culture makes men ashamed of their own inner images, steering them away from the healing potential these fantasies contain. And there is a wide range of what is held to be shameful—not only the destructive, violent, humiliating, and feminizing fantasies, but also the ones in which a man might experience the most loving kind of intimacies.

It is the failure to recognize the value and deeper messages of sexual fantasy, especially the ones he feels ashamed of, that undermines a man's ability to find that which will truly enrich him. And the less he is enriched, the more he will turn to the victimizing and self-victimizing opportunities of exploitative sex. The rehabilitation, in his own eyes, of what a man sees as shameful about his inner sexual world is one of the central healing tasks presented by the problem of sex in the forbidden zone.

WOUNDS FROM THE FATHER: THE LOSS OF INTIMACY IN THE FATHER-SON LEGACY

Although a man's attitude toward sexual fantasy, toward women, and toward himself is shaped to a large degree by cultural values, it is his own father who is usually his preeminent model. Cultural attitudes survive to the degree that they are personally transmitted from father to son. This gives fathers an opportunity to create a new legacy for their sons by modeling values that differ from those of the dominant culture. The current generation of men in power holds in its hands the question of whether the next generation of men will repeat or modify patterns of sexual exploitation that now exist. How men in power mold the father-son legacy when they teach their sons, students, and political, intellectual, and spiritual inheritors will determine these patterns to a greater extent than in the way these men actually relate to women.

Over the years many of my patients have been male professionals who are continually exposed to the sexual temptations of the forbidden zone, whether they have been businessmen, therapists, teachers, lawyers, or clergymen. Almost every one of them has been locked in a struggle to understand his constant battle with the temptations of forbidden sexuality. Some of them had already sexually exploited women in relationships of trust by the time they came to me. Others were looking for a new kind of clarity to help resolve their sexual intoxication in ways that would allow them to pull back from the forbidden boundary. Still others were on the verge of engaging in forbidden-zone sex, did not want to hold back, and were looking to me for any sign of encouragement to go ahead with it.

All of these men, and with rare exceptions all men in our culture, are struggling against a wound caused by the loss of intimacy in the father-son legacy. This significant void provides men with little emotional information when dealing with questions of intimacy. Very few fathers share with their sons anything about their own intimate sexual and emotional experiences. Because these fathers have themselves been taught to hide their vulnerabilities, they are unlikely to have discussed with their sons in a serious way any difficulties they may have had at the boundaries of forbidden sexuality. What will be most hidden is openness about conflicts, doubts, and especially their lapses. This lack of sharing has important consequences that bear directly on what men do and do not learn about their options when confronted with sexual opportunity.

In the absence of a personal connection with a male role-model who is able to provide healthy guidance in matters of intimacy, a man fills the void with information and values from cultural mythology, which is far less personal and is full of caricatures about men and women. According to these caricatures, men receive cultural approval for acting on their sexual tensions, rather than for containing and examining them as inner phenomena. This kind of impersonal cultural stereotyping also fuels the part of the masculine myth of the feminine that attributes both extreme healing and destructive powers to women.

Men's Overdependence on the Feminine for Intimacy

When fathers distance themselves in matters of intimacy, they leave their sons with no way to develop their own inner resources. The life-giving, healing elements that they might have found inside themselves are instead sought out through sexual contact with women. The void in the father-son relationship is filled by dependency on the feminine. This creates a cultural division of labor, in which mothers and other women have been given the task of providing emotional closeness. A boy grows up assuming, without question, that women will continue to be available to him as sources of physical, emotional, and sexual intimacy. When, as a man, he feels a woman is the only available source of intimacy and inner life, it is easy to see how readily he might cross over forbidden sexual boundaries as if it were his right.

Unfortunately, it is nearly impossible for any woman to compensate a man for what has been lost from the father. Yet the culture continues to tell men that they have a right to expect women to take care of the intimate, feeling side of life for them. In a marriage or other intimate relationship, if a woman disappoints a man he is likely to hold her responsible for this deprivation and become angry at her. His anger pushes him even farther away from being able to empathize with her wounds, and he may feel justified in trying to take what he can from her sexually, or to seek what he thinks will be a healing intimacy wherever he can find it. If a man has seen his father and other significant role-models relate to women in this way without questioning it, and has seen women accept such treatment, he will have no other model for his own behavior.

Maintaining Patriarchal Authority at the Expense of Truth

Another terrible loss to men results because fathers spend a great deal of energy establishing and maintaining patriarchal authority over their sons at the expense of sharing matters of intimacy. The effort to maintain authority takes precedence over truth, both emotional and factual. Suppression of truth is seen as necessary to preserving order, and lying becomes an acceptable mode on personal and eventually national and global levels. Without the truth, we become helpless to change anything in our lives and in our world.

The fact that lying has become an acceptable mode in the political arena is reflected in the way male-dominated institutions deal with sexual misconduct by their own members, where truth is often a victim of political considerations. Professional organizations of doctors, therapists, lawyers, and clergy rarely make information about sexual misconduct by their members available to the public for fear that the reputation of the profession itself will be damaged. However, a profession can demonstrate its concern for the public welfare by being open about the activities of its unethical members, thereby enhancing its stature. Some professional organizations are voluntarily evolving toward this position; others will get there only by public pressure and, in some cases, by new legislation that mandates disclosure of sexual and other ethical misconduct.

As it now stands, many religious organizations simply transfer sexually abusive clergy to other locales, with no public admission of misconduct. Health professionals who are discharged from hospital staffs for unethical behavior can move to another state and set up shop there. Because most men who sexually exploit women are repeaters, these men are likely to continue sexually exploiting their positions of power. When doctors, therapists, and lawyers are sued for sexual misconduct, insurance companies will often pay settlements if the injured woman agrees to maintain secrecy about the incident. These agreements are extremely harmful to the effort to fight against sexual exploitation: Not only do they suppress truth, but they are analogous to an incestuous father buying his daughter a gift in return for her silence about their relationship.

In matters of sexual misconduct, men in leadership positions set the ethical tone for society not only in the way they treat women but through the messages they pass on to other men. As symbolic, spiritual, or biological fathers, they are the critical link in the perpetuation—or prevention—of exploitation.

Suppression of truth is harmful in itself. But because it keeps men away from their own inner worlds, it reinforces the personal and cultural dynamics of sexual exploitation. Masculine attitudes will not fundamentally change until different values are passed down by men in power who are role models for the next generation. These values would allow men to tell one another the truth about matters of intimacy and instill respect for sexual fantasy as a point of access for a man's inner resources. Unless we work toward such changes, male leaders will pass on to other men, and to the women they serve, their own wounds.

WOUNDS FROM THE MOTHER: MERGING, DEPRIVATION, AND PLAYING THE VICTIM

Every man's relationship with his mother reaches back to the very origins of his existence, forming the foundation for the life that follows. Although a man's attitudes toward the feminine can be turned negative by the culture and by his father as he grows older, wounds in his childhood relationship to his mother or mother figures can strongly predispose a man toward exploiting women.

The echo of the bond with the mother also helps explain why a man's intimacy with a woman in a forbidden-zone relationship has the power over him that it does. In a curious kind of role reversal, a man in power can come to relate to his female protégée as he might have done with his mother: He becomes the receiver, not the provider, of healing. Even if he is able to feel the pain of the wounded woman/mother, he revels in the warmth of her close presence and the nurturing promise it holds. In this atmosphere, his psyche can easily generate fantasies of recovering with his client or protégée a motherlike quality of intimacy that was injured or lost.

But it is precisely because of this promise of intimacy that danger lurks for a man who carries wounds from the mother into adult forbidden-zone relationships. To the extent that a man has an extra measure of anger toward the feminine, originating from his personal experience of the mother, the power he holds in these relationships of trust gives him the means to avenge himself for injuries that may be reawakened by this promise of intimacy.

I have found three serious psychological liabilities for men in their efforts to maintain healthy sexual boundaries in the forbidden zone that can result from wounds in the relationship between mothers and sons: (1) the disrespect of women's boundaries by men whose mothers were too emotionally merged with their sons; (2) the deprivation and subsequent vengeful anger toward women in men whose mothers were too emotionally distant; and (3) the repeated victimization of women by men who, as boys, saw their mothers do nothing to fight against their own victimization.

The Merged Mother

Mothers who themselves have boundary problems predispose their sons toward later difficulties with sexual-boundary issues. As a child develops from infancy on, he needs appropriate levels of closeness and distance from the mother. The balance between closeness and distance a child needs when he is six months old is very different from what he needs when he is two or six. But at each age the mother must take care at the boundary to neither merge with, invade, nor deprive her child.

No matter how close and loving the bond between mother and infant, the child's psychological health is compromised to the degree that his mother does not see him as a separate being. A mother can easily lose a sense that there is any boundary at all between herself and her child. From the very beginning she may treat him as if they are one unit, keeping physical separation to an absolute minimum.

But what is more significant is the degree of psychological merging that can result. A mother may truly conceive of herself and her child as one merged being. She may decide for him when he is hungry or sleepy, when he should be happy or sad, how far away from her he should toddle—all discouraging the development of his separateness and sense of an independent self. This stunting of autonomy may continue far beyond the toddler stage.

The resulting adult may harbor a profound anger toward the feminine for having made him so powerless. In situations of intimacy with women, this anger and the need to fight against a perceived lack of power can combine, leading to sexually exploiting the power a position of trust grants him. In addition, because his earliest model of closeness was based on merger and the nonexistence of psychological boundaries, he is at high risk to repeat this pattern by taking advantage of the feelings of merger available through a sexual experience.

A merged mother may also passively allow the infant to determine everything in his world, so that she provides no adult guidance to balance the desires of, say, an eighteen-month-old in determining the rhythm of daily life—what to eat, when to sleep, when to spend time alone, when to toddle off independently, which objects are to smash or put in one's mouth, how other people's bodies and property are to be respected. When he is angry, sad, or helpless, so is she; they are consumed together by whatever feeling state he is in.

A child brought up in this way will have been taught that the world is a place in which no boundary exists between his feeling states and the physical and psychological space of other people. A man who carries this world-view will have difficulty believing that a woman from whom he wants something might have a completely different set of needs from his own. In a position of power, such a man will have little hesitation about crossing forbidden sexual boundaries if what he wants lies on the other side.

The Depriving Mother

The depriving mother, on the other hand, is much too emotionally separate from her child. She shares neither his happiness nor his pain. She lets him cry alone, without supplying comfort; she ignores his joyous discoveries about himself and the world around him. As he grows older, his emotional life may become deadened because of the lack of her involvement in it. If a mother does not to some degree anticipate her child's pain, but only involves herself in his emotional life after he has lost control of himself, she is encouraging a pattern in which he may become wild and destructive in his desperation to win a response.

A child whose pain has been ignored is likely to have extremely low self-esteem. As he struggles to understand why the world is not interested in what he feels, and especially in his pain, he concludes that who he is and how he feels must not be very important.

Some mothers who ignore the emotional pain of their children may themselves be so injured that they have become anesthetized to their own feelings. Others are wracked by constant storms of painful feelings that so preoccupy them that there is nothing left with which to reach out to their children. Under these circumstances, a mother may enlist her son in a healing role, overinvolving him in her emotional life and not letting him achieve adequate separation from her pain. She can be both merged and distant at the same time.

If a child has been brought inside his mother's wounded feelings as her healing hope, as an adult he will be predisposed to become closely enmeshed with women's wounds, often at the expense of developing his own emotional separateness.

Consciously or unconsciously, he may be resentful of this bond, yet unable to break it. Men in this pattern both abuse women and allow themselves to be abused. Because these men have a well-developed capacity for taking care of the wounded feminine, they often find their way to careers in the helping professions where they will again be in the role of healer to women.

But the nature of this kind of bond to the wounded feminine puts these men at high risk for sexual-boundary violations. Although their nurturing capacities may be well developed, that development has taken place under conditions in which they were exploited. This model is easily repeated under the intimate conditions of the forbidden zone. Men who have felt overwhelmed and exploited by their duty to take care of the wounded feminine may try to retaliate by asserting their sexual power over vulnerable women.

Dr. William Rin, who described the depression he hoped to escape by having a sexual relationship with his patient, responded this way when I asked him about his relationship with his mother:

> My mother was very depressed. She must have started telling me about problems she had with my father when I was eight or nine, but made me promise not to tell him anything. This made me angry, because I didn't get enough of my father as it was, and this secret knowledge drove a farther wedge between us. On the other hand, when I was unhappy about something, my mother would retreat behind her closed door, saying she felt ill or exhausted.
>
> The day I became sexually involved with my patient, I had been haunted by the fear that she would leave my office, shut the door behind her, and never come back. That was how I so often felt as a child, so I couldn't stand the thought of it happening again. I was so wrapped up in my

pain that I could not even consider how injurious to her it might be to have sexual contact with me.

Dr. Rin's story illustrates a prevalent pattern in men who sexually exploit relationships of trust. These men, whose pain was ignored by their mothers, become emotionally starved. As a result they use the sexual opportunity of the forbidden zone not simply to retaliate but to try desperately to get some nourishment from a woman. In addition, because their self-esteem is low, such men may be so depressed that they feel they have little to lose in terms of behavior that violates ethical standards and puts their professional and personal lives in jeopardy. In this sense, a sexual-boundary violation may be a self-destructive cry for help from the wounded man.

The Mother as Victim: Modeling Abusive Relationships to the Son

Another wound to a man that turns him toward victimizing women is the childhood experience of having observed his mother accept abusive treatment from men. A boy in this position is caught in a destructive crosscurrent from which there is little chance of escape. On the one hand, he identifies and empathizes with his injured mother much as he may be angry with her for her powerlessness and failure to protect herself. On the other hand, he begins to identify with the abusiveness of the father or father figure because, much as he might hate it, at least this role promises to confer some power on him as a man in intimate relationships.

The scenario for teaching children to become victimizers of others is played out through direct modeling from one or both depressed, angry, abusive, and victimized parents. Internalized by a child from the first year of life as an acceptable way to handle emotions, it can be in place by the time a child is four years old. As long as he sees the adults in his world discharge anger and depression by creating victims or by victimizing themselves, the child will learn to do the same.

Whether the victim is the child himself, another member of the family, or someone outside the family, the message of hopelessness will be the same: Because there are no other ways to deal with pain, anger, and depression, you can discharge it on someone else. When children begin school or move outside the family into the social milieu, the patterns from the family begin to blend with the prevailing cultural messages. Boys are then preferentially turned toward victimizing others, while the girls become their victims.

There are healthy, constructive ways to deal with emotional pain. What a child needs in order to develop a hopeful message about dealing with his own pain is a measure of respectful empathy from the adults around him, especially his parents. But some parents were, as children, themselves given so little of this empathy that they become overwhelmed by feelings of helplessness if they cannot readily make a child's pain go away. They have not learned the fundamental point that acknowledging and caring about a child's pain, not making it disappear, is the healthiest possible response.

A mother who feels helpless and overwhelmed can easily become angry at herself and at her child. Such a parent, by ignoring the child's inner states, blaming the child for his pain, or treating him as if his emotional life is too burdensome to deal with, perpetuates and models an abusive way of dealing with emotional injury.

Mothers do not have to resolve or fully escape their roles as victims in order to give their children a healthier model. Women in abusive relationships who simply *begin* the process of questioning their victimization can send a message of hope that the legacy of victimization will not be passed on continually from generation to generation.

Whether a man's compassion for suffering has been invaded and exploited or else hardened by parents who ignored his own pain, he is likely to be truly confused about which side of the forbidden-zone boundary contains the hope for healing—his own, or on the other side in the body and psyche of the woman.

4

Women in the Forbidden Zone: Stages in the Betrayal of Hope

Dolores Vance, a psychologist in her late forties, experienced the following dream:

A man took me to see his home in the wine country. It was an old rustic wooden house, which seemed enchanted. It looked small, but as we went from room to room, space opened out in front of us. The rooms themselves began to glow deeply in intensity, color, light, dimension, and were all exquisitely appointed. Out the windows I could see nothing but rolling green fields and vineyards.

He gave me a cognac to try whose taste was the epitome of the warm, cultivated excellence of the house. The taste was indescribably wonderful: unusual, deep, and strong. The house was quiet and ordinary, not splendid; but a glow and special feeling emerged as we wandered through it, and it took on a cathedral-like ambiance.

The man had a mate; he showed me their bedroom. There, he gave me a minute sample of a red wine in a shot glass. It had a musky, grape taste and a slight, bitter, dry aftertaste that made it exquisite and unusual. I was thinking how I would tell him that I did not want to sleep with him, because what I really wanted was the friendship with him, and sexuality would spoil it.

No matter how wounded a woman may be, a fantasy of hope awakens in her when she enters a forbidden-zone relationship of trust with a man. The special qualities that these relationships carry for healing the past and opening the future come into play the moment a woman walks in the door and sits down in the physical presence of her male therapist, mentor, pastor, or lawyer. Her hope is for, among other things, a rich and expanding relationship between herself and the outside world. And the man sitting across from her at this moment in her life has the power either to undermine her or help her find her own strength.

The factors that generate the feminine fantasy of hope are well in place long before the forbidden-zone relationship actually begins. This is because almost all women carry around, in their inner worlds, the image of a man who will usher them into a larger sense of life.

THE FANTASY OF HOPE: INNER IMAGES OF MEN

Dolores Vance's work focuses on helping women recover dimensions of their femininity that the culture has discouraged them from expressing. The dream she told me helps illustrate components of feminine psychology that make forbidden-zone relationships both so valuable and so dangerous. The key to the dream is the power of the man to symbolize simultaneously both her hopes and the threat of forbidden sexuality.

In Dr. Vance's dream, the man who brings her into his house is not anyone she actually knows. Instead, he is a depiction of her *inner* image of a powerful, beneficent masculine force. He embodies her fantasy of hope, her wish that parts of her that have never been expressed will, like the rich red wine he serves her, reach fruition. The expanded sense of aliveness that a man can evoke in a woman is expressed when the man takes her into his house and offers her the cognac, in rooms opening out and glowing with light.

In a woman's fantasy of hope, the man often carries the power to recognize who she is and to help her develop her capabilities so that they can be manifested in the outside world. This kind of recognition from a man also gives him the power to help develop her inner sense of self-esteem.

Dr. Vance, a recognized expert in the field of feminine psychology, shares with us her perspective that the powerful masculine images in women's psyches have dimensions of meaning beyond simply reexperiencing the power their fathers and other men had in their lives:

> Women's inner images of men have to do with the fact that men embody the unknown, the opposite of ourselves. These masculine images are natural parts of us, not just cultural aberrations.
>
> In my dream, the man is an inner guide. He is not attractive or important as himself, but for his cultivation with respect to wine and "spirits." The distilled essence he gives me to taste is the essence of spirituality. He has this to share with me, and through this sharing, the house, representing my own growth, becomes ever-expanding. For me, everything is in order in this dream. There is no Dionysian abandon, no drunkenness. The man represents the epitome of cultivated masculine sensibility. I feel as if I have something to learn through tasting—just tasting—these distilled essences, and I know that sexuality has no part in it.

Women experience the inner presence of this masculine force in a variety of ways. Sometimes they perceive it purely as a feeling, an intuition of the power a man could have for her, with no actual image in the shape of a man involved. Other women have daydreams or waking fantasies that generate images of men, which may or may not resemble men they have ever seen. Such images can be ever-changing or can return repeatedly to the figure of one particular man.

There is no danger to a woman simply because she experiences powerful masculine images. The liability lies in her failure to understand that the power conveyed in images of men is *her own*. If she understands that ultimately this power is hers, she will be able to extricate herself from a relationship with a man who fails to act as a trustworthy guide.

The greatest risk arises when a woman feels that the power symbolized by her masculine images really does belong to men in her life. She can fall completely under the spell of a powerful man, especially when her inner fantasy of hope becomes fixated on a man whom she knows personally or through media images, leading her to believe that her entire future depends upon having an intimate connection with him.

Adolescent girls are especially vulnerable to bestowing on men in the public eye, such as popular musicians, godlike qualities of power that they then devote their lives to worshipping. At best, a young woman will withdraw this power from the man she worships and come to feel some of it as potential strength in her own personality. At worst, an adolescent intoxication may demonstrate that a woman has already developed a pattern, which she will repeat, of submitting herself to a series of powerful men.

Whether a woman will be able to claim her own strength depends a great deal on how her experience of masculine power is interpreted back to her in childhood. If her male and female role models encourage her to locate strength in men rather than in herself, she will be steered away from developing her own capabilities.

Forbidden-zone relationships intensely reenact for women their childhood power dynamics with men. A male therapist, pastor, or teacher may be the first man in her life who listens to her, encourages her, and teaches her how to develop her own strength. When a woman feels from a man this enlivening quality of recognition for who she really is, her fantasy of hope begins to be fulfilled and she endows their relationship with immeasurable value. The beauty of such relationships is that when a man lives up to his role as the woman's protector, healing moments occur that allow her to continue developing herself.

Dr. Vance's dream, which embodies so many qualities of strength, also depicts the danger lurking in relationships of immeasurable value. The dream ends as the man leads her to his bedroom, posing the yet-unanswered question of whether she can have all the richness embodied in their connection without a sexual relationship. This critical question must be asked and answered in each forbidden-zone relationship: Can it be maintained at a level of intimate, healing contact, or will sexual contact become the price of continuing the relationship?

When a relationship offers a woman fulfillment of her deepest expressions of self, she will go to great extremes to maintain it. The man often comes to represent realized, not just fantasized, hope. All subsequent events leading to sex in the forbidden zone are built upon this psychological foundation.

SEEKING CONNECTION

When a woman by desperation, happenstance, or choice sits down with a man in a forbidden-zone relationship, some part of her immediately begins searching for signs of whether he will fulfill her fantasy of hope. Her wound and her hope are stirred, often more intensely than she realizes. She searches for a connection with the real man in the room with her, who in some ways is modeled on her inner image of what a man can offer. Her seeking of connection begins before they meet—in a phone call making an appointment, in entering his waiting room, in hearing about him from other people. It intensifies as she walks into his office. When the door closes, she starts to track what is happening between them both physically and psychologically, directing her attention to the man as an emanation of hope. Will the hope he represents reach across empty space and connect with her?

She looks to his eyes and listens to his words. Does he see her, or is he absorbed in his own world? Do his words feel as if they are meant for her personally, or is he treating her as a "type"? The more she feels he sees and values her for who she is, the more her hope is stirred, making it likely she will want this relationship to grow and continue.

If she perceives little connection, little eye contact, a non-specific response to her words, then feelings of emptiness and loss will replace hope. She is, once more, left alone and unseen. But because so many different emotions arise under these circumstances, the distinction between what does or does not constitute a promising connection is rarely clear, even in women with exquisite judgment.

For example, Helen Kifner, the attorney whose articulation of betrayed hope was addressed in chapter 1, has a very clear sense of boundaries. Her story of sex in the forbidden zone demonstrates that even women of great professional accomplishment can lose their more adult abilities to distinguish real help from exploitative invasion, especially when a relationship of trust touches a wound that reaches back to childhood:

> I entered therapy with him very much from the "vulnerable daughter" side, with an enormous amount of dependency. But I hid this dependency by my need to appear independent and competent at all times.
>
> So the dependent, alone, inner child was hidden from everyone I knew—even from myself. But it jumped right out as soon as Dr. Yount appeared to be interested in it. He was so good, so practiced at simulating true interest, and of

course the child in me was so needy I took his interest to be genuine. It wasn't until much later that I realized he was not interested in me, only in what he could get for himself.

Helen Kifner's vulnerability to sex in the forbidden zone is echoed by a great many healthy, successful women. The way these relationships reawaken childhood needs and wounds helps explain why women often lose the capability of exercising adult choice.

Women who come from emotionally deprived backgrounds are so vulnerable to any glimmer of awakened hope that they are unable to leave, no matter how faint or compromised a connection they feel, and are in danger of accepting the continuation of a relationship on virtually any terms the man sets.

Sharon Grant, for example, a painter in her fifties who had been sexually molested as a child, engaged in a year-long affair with her attorney while he was representing her in a divorce. She remembers feeling flattered when he originally propositioned her, despite also feeling revulsion toward him for asking:

You have to understand that I was as depressed as I could be. My husband had left me after tearing me down for years. My self-esteem was completely gone. I was forty-seven. My economic future and actual survival were completely dependent on how my lawyer handled my case. He was being very positive about the outcome. When he first came on to me, something in me responded, but I think it was to the protection and hope he represented, not the sexuality.

He wanted our relationship to be sexual, and his desire decided it for me. I had never been given any examples of how to push back against men. I was raised by a fairly cold mother and a stepfather who abused me and used to "feel me up" when I was a child. I was so weak and threatened that I interpreted my lawyer's pass as a positive gesture toward me.

For many women who eventually have sex in the forbidden zone, the wish for connection originates in the hope for restoration of a lost father-daughter (or even mother-daughter) bond. Because these wishes arise from an age when nonsexual kisses and embraces flow naturally as the expression of parental love, a woman who feels a reawakening of hope with a man may wish to touch him or be touched by him. It is precisely at this point that the man in authority is supposed to stand guard against the illusion that anything constructive can come from expressing childhood wishes for touching through the adulthood medium of sexuality.

Whatever the woman's deprivation from the past, it must be healed in a way that brings her into the present and her future. For this to take place, she may seek and receive from the man the most intimate and personal sense of connection, as long as it is expressed psychologically and nonpossessively. This kind of closeness provides a woman with a quality of intimacy that truly nurtures her own emerging aliveness. But sexual behavior takes that aliveness from her and turns it toward ministering to the man's injured self.

NEEDING TO FEEL SPECIAL

Feelings of connection and specialness are inseparable. Any connection implies some degree of specialness, and the connection grows stronger the more a woman feels that she is being treated specially. At the beginning of a forbidden-zone relationship, the fact that she is alone with the man awakens in the woman the promise that this man will recognize and give life to her unique qualities.

In Dolores Vance's dream, this initial level of connection is expressed when the man takes her into his house. This alone makes her feel less restricted. The expanses of light, color, dimension, and space that she feels are really qualities of her own expanded inner self, being given to her through a relationship with a man. But an enormous leap in the level of connectedness and specialness takes place when Dolores drinks the proffered cognac. She feels the taste to be "indescribably wonderful—unusual, deep, and strong." This represents the experience of a woman in a forbidden-zone relationship who feels the man in power is listening to her, trying to understand her injury or her potential, and showing a willingness to bear with her and help her. When this kind of relationship is offered by a man, its emotional "taste" is, in fact, "indescribably wonderful."

A woman's quest for special connection is based on her need to heal not only visible outer problems but also her relation to her inner self. A woman can heal both inside and outside when she is offered what she may have had in short supply in her family and cultural environment: a rich and nonexploitative entry into the world of the masculine.

The feminine quest for specialness, and how it can go wrong, can be traced in the experience of Kirsten Breland, a thirty-nine-year-old professor of history who relates the entangled sexual relationship she had with her psychiatrist:

I had started seeing Dr. Noren when I first taught classes in graduate school. I was so anxious and wired about appearing in front of students and failing that I couldn't eat and was afraid I would have to quit in failure. He was charismatic and bright, and I was immediately attracted to his mind and his seeming control of things.

At first, when we were still just doing therapy, he was very helpful and got me calmed down so I could do my job, for which I was enormously grateful. I started getting into deeper issues, such as my relationships with men, and I began feeling quite dependent on him. His office hours were from 3 P.M. to midnight, and he often slept weeknights in his office instead of going back to his wife and children in the suburbs. One night after I had been in treatment with him for about three months, he called me at eleven o'clock at night and asked me if I'd like to come back and talk more about my problems of self-image with men, which we had been dealing with in therapy. I remember having told him that I had no confidence in my attractiveness to men when my clothes were on, but I felt more comfortable with them sexually with my clothes off.

I went back late that night. Dr. Noren asked me this very well-thought-out question about whether I would like to go to bed with him. He presented it purely as a matter of choice for me. It had been absolutely the last thing in my mind, but I had no objection when he brought it up. In fact, I was very flattered and thought this was a wonderful idea. So we slept together on the spot.

Now I see there was no possibility that I could have said no. Absolutely none. I was just together enough that I would have to say yes. The opportunity to have such a special relationship with this man who meant so much to me was something I absolutely could not turn down.

That is how it started. I would see him once or twice a week in his office-apartment. Often we would have a therapy session, end it at eleven at night, and then just go on to the sexual relating. I had been sleeping with him, while remaining his patient, for three months, innocently thinking how wonderful and special it all was. My problem came when he announced to me that we should stop sleeping together and that I should go back to being just his patient. I found this extremely painful. I took it as both a rebuke and a test. From then on, I spent the entire course of our therapy figuring out what I had done wrong, and how I could become a good enough patient so he would start sleeping with me again. It became the dominant theme in my life.

In staying in therapy with him after we stopped sleeping together and in trying to be his star pupil so he'd sleep with me again, I tore down whatever shreds of self-respect I had had. The therapy was bad for me in other ways as well. He believed that you could think your way out of anything. Nothing could have been more disastrous for me. I was totally out of touch with my feelings anyway and didn't need reinforcement of a perspective that emphasized thoughts over feelings.

I finally decided that I'd confront him about sleeping with patients, which I knew he was still doing. But he just threw it back on me, telling me that it was my problem that I couldn't handle it. I finally left therapy with him, seeing that this was very destructive to me. But things did not get any better. I went through a deep depression. I started to feel a little better when I completed my doctorate. I was angry at him, but when our relationship came up in conversation with a few friends of mine, I still defended him. At that point I still couldn't admit to the loss of all I had put into that relationship. If I said that he was no good, I felt that I was really attacking myself. I couldn't admit that I had been injured. Although I felt it, admitting it at that point would have been a bigger injury.

Gradually, I have developed real anger and outrage at what happened. I finally realized I had had no opportunity to say no to his sexual invitation. It was just his myth that I had acquiesced to him. I had had no other choice. When I felt angry I could see myself as a victim rather than as a stupid participant.

Kirsten Breland achieved, then painfully lost, what seems at times to express for women the ultimate realization of their specialness: sexual involvement with a man in power. There

is little doubt that many women are prisoners of this syndrome. They feel lost and empty without such liaisons, and
repeatedly, sometimes aggressively, seek them out as their
own kind of sexual conquest. Yet the sexual relationship does
nothing to remedy the inner emptiness. When it occurs in the
forbidden zone with a man who has a responsibility not to let
it happen, a woman inevitably leaves the sexual relationship
with more damage than when she entered it.

REVEALING THE FEMININE CORE: CONFUSION
BETWEEN SEXUAL AND NONSEXUAL

If her fantasy of hope is being received by the man, a woman
will open herself still farther. She will peel away more and
more layers of herself, revealing to him and allowing herself
to experience an urgent onrush of feelings that she had long
suppressed. As the warming of intimacy continues, the un-
folding can reach to the core of a woman's being. Her hidden
thoughts, feelings, wounds, and aspirations are now brought
to the man, told to him, or felt, silently, in his presence. This
is a sacred and dangerous condition. Her spirit reaches out to
him, and his to her. Even a woman with a firm sense of boundaries in other kinds of relationships may well stop guarding
them so that her core may be seen and known by this man. A
man who is invested with this special level of trust needs to
guard against misinterpreting as sexual the deeply passionate
ways a woman may express herself when she responds to his
promise of acceptance.

Helen Kifner describes this extraordinary state when she
speaks of revealing her core to her doctor in the months
preceding their sexual relationship: "There is no doubt that
what I felt was an almost indescribable combination of erotic-
spiritual intensity. I felt as if Dr. Yount almost physically had
touched my heart. It was an ecstatic experience."

When a woman has been touched to her core, she may

temporarily lose her sense of differentiation between what is sexual and what is nonsexual. The passion for life itself that she is discovering in this state can be mistaken by the man, or even by the woman, as a call for a sexual exchange between them.

Patricia Elmont, now a psychologist, describes the way her therapist redirected her nonsexual passion toward his own sexual needs. Patricia was twenty-six and the mother of two children when her husband's job necessitated a move far away from the community in which she had grown up. The move intensified the depression she already had been feeling, and so she began psychotherapy.

At first, Dr. Thomas Stuben awakened in Patricia the hope that, through his example and guidance, she could find a creative outlet for her bottled-up energy. But her passion to develop herself as someone other than a housewife turned out to be easily diverted into sexual behavior:

> Thomas excited me immediately with his ideas and intellect. I had a tremendous passion for religious understanding, but no place to put it. I knew this was the real source of my depression. He was very supportive of me. In fact, he was the first man who really seemed excited by my mind, rather than my body. Although I knew he was carrying tremendous spiritual power for me, I couldn't separate it from the sexual. I was so excited by what was going on that I started developing erotic fantasies about him.

Patricia felt her sexual feelings posed no danger, because she assumed she was protected by the fact that Dr. Stuben was her therapist. She could continue to feel the healing power of her admittedly eroticized intellectual awakening, knowing that sexual behavior was out of the question.

She was surprised, then, when the boundaries of professional distance became gradually blurred. First, Dr. Stuben invited Patricia and her husband to a party at his home. Soon afterward, he asked her to drive him to a lecture he was giving. Later he backed off from the idea of their driving together, because, as he told her, "We might not be able to keep our hands off each other." This suggestive remark devastated Patricia. It deprived her of the protection she needed at a time when her own boundaries between sexual and nonsexual passion were unclear. From that moment, she knew that he saw her as a possible sexual conquest and that all of his responses toward her were compromised by his attempt to seduce her. In her confusion, she found that Dr. Stuben's sexually explicit comment only increased her sexual fantasizing, which tormented her because she knew how wrong it would be to have sex with him.

But soon afterward, just as she had expected, Dr. Stuben proposed, during a therapy hour, that they have intercourse.

I felt incapable of doing anything that might disappoint him. So of course I couldn't say no. It never occurred to me to say no. I was horribly lonely and depressed, and by now I had become totally dependent on him for any chance of expressing myself.

Patricia went along with it, and for a year had sexual relations in his office during her twice-weekly therapy hours. She maintained strict secrecy, unwilling, indeed incapable, of doing anything to jeopardize her connection to him.

A year later her husband was again transferred, and this ended the relationship. Patricia became even more depressed but felt she could not possibly reenter therapy because of what had previously occurred. Her marriage broke up, the final blow coming when she confessed to her husband the nature of her relationship with her former therapist. Despite a satisfying second marriage, Patricia still feels the pain and damage:

It's really criminal that he didn't help me discover where to put this passion of life coming out of me. I felt this intense, burning, despairing longing that never got dealt with. The most awful part about it was how he exploited and damaged my emerging life-energy.

I felt very depressed after each time we had sex. But I'm not sure, after all this time, that I've really looked at how damaging that sexual relationship was. At its best, therapy can help someone discover her inner passion and help channel it into a meaningful life's work. He destroyed that possibility in me for a very long time. I'm a pretty tough person. I didn't die from it, and I have for the most part recovered. But he took at least ten years of my life away from me that I had to devote to getting over the damage. It was really evil.

The fullness of feminine passion that Patricia Elmont brought her therapist is typical of what powerful men can awaken for women in forbidden-zone relationships. If the woman loses her sense of boundaries because she is touched to the core, only the man will be in a position to uphold the prohibition against sexuality. But the man's own fantasy life is likely to be stimulated by his involvement with a woman who has revealed her psychological core. Under these circumstances, he must be especially vigilant not to allow the sexual boundary between them to be dissolved.

DISSOLVING THE BOUNDARY

Once the deepest feelings in a woman touch a man at his own core, both of them can lose touch with the reality that their relationship is bound by professional rules. A human level of connection is experienced that transcends the professional roles of the man-as-healer and the woman-as-wounded.

When he is in this frame of mind, the man may feel that his professional responsibility stands in the way of his own fulfillment and wish with all his heart to relinquish his power role, participating instead as the wounded one, able to partake of the healing feminine qualities he experiences in the woman. And the woman, adapted to offer her femininity to men's wounds, may feel all the more obligated to offer this balm to the man in return for what he has done for her. This mutually dissolving quality of deep connection frequently occurs in the forbidden zone.

At this point, the cultural messages that allow men to ignore boundaries against sexual intimacy can come into play. The man has been invested not only with power over the woman's inner state but with the authority to set the rules of their relationship. This means that he not only controls the physical boundary but is also in the position of redefining the very concept of boundaries to the woman. Frequently this involves his telling her that sexual contact is not forbidden by their professional relationship, such as when a therapist tells a patient that having sex is part of her treatment or a mentor tells a protégée that it is part of her education.

This was played out when Reverend Clifton told Ruth Smythlin that their sexual relationship was part of her pastoral training, and that her ability to keep it secret was a measure of her spiritual development and commitment to the church community. Ruth had begun studying for the ministry at a small midwestern seminary after graduating from college on the East Coast. She was then twenty-one. Soon after she arrived, Reverend Clifton, a married man with five children who was dean of the seminary, took a special interest in her:

> When he offered me a job as his personal assistant, requiring intimate daily contact, I remember getting a sick feeling in my stomach about my giving him so much power over my life. But he was offering me the fulfillment of a dream

I had always had of a very special kind of recognition, so I pushed away my feeling that it was wrong.

Soon afterward, Reverend Clifton made it clear that her special position required her to be sexually available to him. Ruth complied, for reasons she still has trouble comprehending, and began a secret, five-year sexual relationship. Reverend Clifton, a nationally prominent religious educator, insisted on complete secrecy because his world would have been destroyed had their affair been revealed.

Because of the secrecy, Ruth recounts how she moved progressively farther from the religious community to which she had wanted to devote her life:

I felt total isolation, because I could not speak to anyone about this relationship. If I only could have had more trust in myself. I still feel ashamed that I didn't act very quickly against this at the beginning. This was a very sick relationship, but I was committed to it.

Ruth finally broke off the relationship when it became clear that he was abusing his pastoral power by having sexual relationships with other women. Terrified, she continued to maintain silence about his sexual misconduct. Although she was finally ordained by him, she describes it as a completely empty experience. Ruth is now thirty. She has moved far away from the community in which she had felt such promise. Much of the life seems to have gone out of her, and she despairs of ever getting it back:

As it turned out, my relationship with Reverend Clifton was so destructive not primarily because of my sexual enslavement, but because he further decimated my trust in myself and deepened my own self-hatred. I violated myself by attempting to trust him more than myself. It's so hard to talk about this that I have just bottled it up for the last seven years. I can't tell you how painful it is for me to look straight on at how many years of my life sank into that black mire, and really to know that I'm not over it.

Ruth was, and remains, a sophisticated and socially conscious woman. Her vulnerability to accepting Reverend Clifton's definitions of their sexual boundary did not come from naiveté but from the fact that she had revealed her core with him and had been taught, within her family and our culture, to adapt herself to the moral and spiritual authority of men.

FEELING AMBIVALENCE: PARTICIPATION AND REVULSION

Women grasp their fantasies of hope in the forbidden zone as assiduously as men cling to their fantasies of sexual healing. A woman at this stage demonstrates extreme ambivalence, both recognizing and denying a man's sexual behavior toward her. If he touches her on the way out of the office, she may know it is sexual yet try very hard to see it as a sign of nonsexual caring. If he invites her to meet him outside the office, she can incorporate it into her fantasy that he is showing special recognition for her work and ignore signs that he is being seductive.

Because she wants to trust him and to maintain her image of him as the strong, health-giving professional, a woman can permit a great deal of erosion of boundaries by denying the seductive element in his behavior. If questioned, men often support this by themselves strongly disavowing, even if they have to lie, sexually suggestive aspects of their behavior.

A woman's ambivalence also manifests in her difficulty

distinguishing between invasive and noninvasive caring. A woman who has been deprived of feeling special may welcome any manifestation of intimate connection to the man, even the sexual, as preferable to the alternative of a return to what she perceives as hopeless isolation. Diana Tilton, Barbara Forsch, and Kirsten Breland each welcomed the sexual attention of their therapists at the moment it was offered. Kirsten even admitted that after Dr. Noren ended their sexual relationship she continued therapy in the belief that the sign of her getting "better" would be his wanting to resume sex with her.

Each of these women incorporated into her fantasy of hope the fact that her therapist offered to have sex with her. Women tend to blur the boundary between reality and fantasy by accepting the reality that has been offered without trying to change it, and then fitting it into a preexisting fantasy. On the other hand, men are more likely to demand that people change their behavior until it fits the current fantasy.

When a man and woman begin having sexual contact in the forbidden zone, a woman experiences powerful ambivalence in her conflict between participation and revulsion. When both sides of this conflict are strong, these contradictory feeling states can coexist. A woman participates in the sexual behavior, simultaneously experiencing deep revulsion at her own actions.

Many women report that they felt "nauseated," "sickened," "repulsed," or "degraded" at the very moment when they began an exploitative sexual relationship. Yet they have tended not to act on these feelings when they have had them. It often takes them years to gain the strength to disengage from these relationships, if they ever do. Furthermore, one of the most tragic aspects of feeling revulsion is that the woman almost always turns it against herself. Unable to understand how fully she has been victimized, she turns the blame and subsequent self-hatred on herself.

THE MOMENT OF SEXUAL TOUCHING: PARALYSIS IN THE FACE OF DANGER

When the forbidden boundary is finally dissolved by the moment of sexual touching, a woman experiences a multitude of emotions, blurred together in a disharmonious clamor. At the center of these feelings lies an overwhelming sense of danger. At the deepest level, she knows that a destructive invasion has taken place. Although it may take years, even decades, from the time of the first sexual act for her to become aware of this destructiveness, something in her knows it instantly and fills her with feelings of dread.

At another level, a different danger looms: the threat of losing her connecfion with the man in whose presence she has come to feel some of the specialness she so deeply needs. Overwhelmed and confused by the contradiction between her fear of disappointing or enraging him and a deeper sense of being violated, she is unlikely to have the strength and clarity that it takes to deal effectively with the moment of sexual touching.

The result is paralysis—of action, judgment, feeling, and voice. The cultural messages encouraging passivity, the personal wounds from her family that have shown her there is no protective boundary, the hope that someone will treat her differently all come together as an overwhelming flood at the moment the man touches her. This paralysis can last for minutes, hours, days, and sometimes years. In the meantime, the man has proceeded with his sexual scenario.

At this point, a woman can completely shut down her feelings, dissociating herself from the body that is acting sexually. This split creates a state called "psychic numbing," a term that was first used to describe the effect on people who are completely powerless in the face of overwhelming catastrophe, such as concentration camp internment.

Sharon Grant describes the helplessness leading to psychic

numbing that she felt at the moment her attorney told her he would abandon a lawsuit to keep her house unless she agreed to have sex:

> There was no way to control anything. When this happens, there is no boundary to the self. There is no self. Anybody can do anything he wants to you. You have no power, no control, no choice. You can't say yes or no.

Psychic numbing is a prominent symptom of a medical condition called posttraumatic stress disorder, which victims of sexual abuse—rape, child molestation, and incest—often live with for years. The psychological wounds and subsequent scars of sexual exploitation of the forbidden-zone relationships are remarkably similar.

"I MUST HEAL HIM": ATTEMPTS TO ADAPT TO DESTRUCTIVENESS

At one level, it may appear that a woman participates in sex in the forbidden zone primarily because she hopes to preserve something of immeasurable value: the enlivening specialness that she has come to feel in relationship to her mentor, therapist, pastor, lawyer, or teacher. At a deeper level, however, the danger and powerlessness she feels drive her away from whatever she might need for herself. She turns instead toward adapting to the needs of the man who is exploiting her.

On the surface, she fears the man's rage and unhappiness, and she dreads playing a part in shattering a relationship that has contained so much hope. But beneath the surface, from the beginning, even profoundly wounded women reach out to heal the men who exploit them. This dynamic often has its origins in the father-daughter relationship, exemplified in a pattern frequently present in daughters of alcoholic men. These women learn very early in life to minister to their fathers' illnesses, in the hope of simply keeping them in the house one more day and ultimately in the hope of keeping them alive.

The woman's attempt to heal the wounded man comes strongly into play after sex in the forbidden zone has been consummated. It has the effect of keeping her involved. Although she may have felt his wounds before then, until the sexual barrier has been dissolved the man still retains a semblance of his healing and protective capacity. But in the act of beginning a sexual relationship, the man has destroyed his ability to help her. Instead, he has damaged her with his own wound. Yet because he is more overtly expressing his wound by allowing a sexual relationship, she is pulled all the more strongly into taking care of him. Now he is exploiting more than her spirit and sexuality; he is also exploiting her capacity for compassion.

Feminine compassion, biologically rooted in the instinct for selfless response to an infant, has a tenacity that helps explain why women can allow themselves to be exploited for years, why they go to such lengths to rationalize continuing participation in destructive relationships. This has nothing to do with so-called feminine masochism, which is yet another way that men express the attitude that "she really wanted it." Women's inability to leave abusive relationships is, rather, the result of a conspiracy between their natural instinct to nurture and a culturally accepted role that they have been taught to play and that men expect of them.

In the immediate aftermath of forbidden-zone sex, the woman feels her original wound intensified, along with the death of hope. Although it may take decades for her to appreciate fully the betrayal, loss, and damage emanating from the moment of sexual contact in the forbidden zone, she has in that moment been returned to the state of woundedness in which she entered this man's presence. Furthermore, she has been returned to it with hope itself destroyed. Many women never recover.

5

Men in the Forbidden Zone: Snapshots of a Man Crossing the Boundary

The following sequence of psychological snapshots captures the typical ways in which men convince themselves and their protégées to participate in forbidden-zone sexual relationships. These steps reveal the innermost thoughts, feelings, and strategies of men who cross over the sexual barrier—first by testing it, then by attempting to redefine it, and finally, if necessary, by dispensing with it altogether.

CREATING A PORTRAIT: PSYCHOLOGICAL SNAPSHOTS OF A MAN'S BEHAVIOR

Sex in the forbidden zone begins, imperceptibly to the woman, with a subtle change in a man's attitude toward his sexual fantasies. With this change, he decides that his right to test the potential reality of such fantasies outweighs his duty to keep sex out of the relationship with his protégée. His sexual interest in her, initially relegated to his fantasy world, begins increasingly to intrude itself into the physical and psychological space they share. He behaves differently toward her, testing in many different ways whether she will accept his secret redefinition of their relationship as one that might include sexual contact. With each step, the man convinces himself, and hopes to convince the woman, that prohibitions on sexuality in relationships of trust can be ignored.

The behavior I describe in these psychological snapshots form a consensus portrait that is based on my many years of observing the darker, exploitative side of the masculine mind in action—in friends, patients, colleagues, and at times in myself. Not all steps occur in every situation or necessarily in the order presented. A man can take months or years to progress from his initial fantasy to actual sexual contact. He may skip steps, or he may fly through all of the stages in a few minutes. Because men have a terrific amount of energy and ingenuity that gets directed toward sexual pursuit, any list of steps at best represents typical patterns, but it is by no means complete.

Men who read this chapter may be able to recognize themselves moving in a direction that endangers both themselves and the woman involved; they should remember that they can choose at any moment to change course and relinquish their sexual agenda. Women who read this chapter can learn what goes on inside men that allows them to sexualize relationships that should remain nonsexual. More specific suggestions for the ways women and men can stop relationships that are headed toward sexual exploitation are contained in chapters 7 and 8.

These snapshots are harsh portrayals; at times they may seem so extreme as to resemble caricatures. Yet this is how men really think when they are in the grip of the misguided expressions of sexuality that characterize sex in the forbidden zone. Intoxicated by their fantasies, they lose their best qualities of self and *become* caricatures.

Yet men have so much more to offer women in forbidden-zone relationships. To balance the darker side of masculine sexual behavior about to be portrayed, this chapter concludes with a summary of the caring and compassionate side of masculine psychology.

Although I present these portraits from the point of view of the man in power, it is important to remember that each step he takes generates a corresponding invasive effect on the psyche of the woman in his presence, activating in her the feeling states described in the previous chapter.

I'm looking her over.   Men bring their everyday sexual instincts with them when they enter the forbidden zone, regardless of rules that prohibit sexual behavior. Scrutinizing a woman in order to evaluate sexual possibilities is a basic male instinct. Yet looking a woman over is not in itself inherently exploitative if a man can keep this instinctive activity to himself. On the other hand, men can look at women in ways so obviously suggestive that they constitute invasive behavior that is completely unacceptable in a forbidden-zone relationship.

I wonder if she's interested in me.   A man who is interested in a woman becomes very concerned with the degree to which his interest is being reciprocated. He closely monitors any signals from the woman for signs of her interest in him. At this stage, a man may begin diverting his attention from his role as a woman's teacher, healer, or mentor because of his preoccupation with the question of whether she is attracted to him.

I wonder what she'd be like to touch.   Although at this stage a man is still wondering rather than acting, his fantasy life is becoming more developed. He may begin running through a series of fantasies about his protégée in which they somehow end up having sexual contact. To a degree, this fantasy activity is a nearly universal aspect of normal masculine psychology, in and out of the forbidden zone. The challenge to a man at this stage remains keeping his fantasies completely to himself and not changing his behavior toward the woman in question to serve his fantasy life.

I can't stop fantasizing about her when I'm away from her. Despite his intensifying involvement, fantasizing about a woman in her absence can actually help protect her from exploitation. As a man becomes more preoccupied with his fantasy, the farther *away* from the real woman that he takes her image the better, even if he thinks about her in masturbatory fantasies. If a man can admit to himself that he is becoming obsessed with a woman, he may also be able to recognize that he has to work at guarding their relationship from becoming sexual.

Through his fantasy, the man has created an inner image of the woman that he can use when he is separated from her. At this critical stage, he may need the help of a friend, mentor, or therapist so that he can continue to redirect his obsession away from the woman herself and toward discovering what her image represents to him. If he does not make this distinction, he may use the fantasies he has at home to fuel his invasiveness and to make more concrete plans for crossing the sexual barrier.

I'll ask her about her sex life. We often assume that this highly intimate question is a legitimate one when a doctor, therapist, pastor, or lawyer asks it of a woman whose sex life is relevant to their work together. Yet professional men often use this legitimacy as a pretext for their own curiosity. When a man inquires about a woman's sexual life because it serves his fantasy about her, he is already beginning to exploit her.

I'll ask her whether she has fantasies about me. This is a more personalized version of the previous question. Many psychotherapists assume that asking patients to report their sexual fantasies is necessary in order to conduct therapy. Yet among therapists and men in other professions it is often a certain indication of their intention to probe the boundaries of the relationship.

For a man to ask a woman to disclose her fantasies about him is highly suggestive and can be used as an invitation for her to reveal what he hopes to find: that she is sexually attracted to him. Asking this question represents a proposition in disguise. When a man does this, he is already endangering her by blurring the distinction between his responsibility toward the woman and the needs of his sexual fantasy world.

I'll begin to close the physical space between us and see how she reacts. Until this stage, the man has been psychologically rather than physically invasive. He may begin his physical invasion by standing closer to the woman than normal social space warrants. A strong theme in the sexual fantasy life of men is that a woman will suddenly find him irresistibly attractive and will respond to his nonverbal approaches with her own counterapproaches, leading to a wordless, sudden sexual encounter. Although at this stage a man may only be "testing" the woman's responses by standing nearer to her, he is perilously close to giving in to his underlying sexual wishes.

He continues to test the woman's response to his fantasy through subtle or blatant physical acts. He may "accidentally" brush against her, put his hand on her shoulder as an act of ostensible politesse, or resort to hugging and other touching as a sign of "openness." A man vigilantly monitors a woman's response to each of these acts, searching for a sign that she reciprocates his sexual desire.

At this stage a man may be collecting more material for his private fantasy life, or else he may be analyzing the woman's responses as part of his plans for further sexual invasion. He may also be rehearsing in his mind the ultimate fantasy: that the subtlest sexual hint from him will cause them both to surrender to their mutual sexual passion, right here, right now.

I'll become more overtly suggestive, hoping she will respond. Now escalating his behavior, the man becomes more daring and physically invasive. He adds verbally suggestive behavior to his arsenal, although he may continue to use ambiguity to disguise his sexual provocativeness, hoping to lay a basis for claiming that the woman "misunderstood" his gestures as being sexual if things do not work out. Despite his wish to maintain ambiguity, a man's behavior at this stage can be quite explicit. He will extend the range of his hugs and other incidental touching, perhaps letting his hands "accidentally" slide over her breasts. He may posture his own body into increasingly frank sexual poses, and begin touching himself on or near his genitals.

He may begin commenting, under the guise of neutral observation or warm support, about how attractive she is. He might "joke" that he would be interested in her himself if it weren't for the fact that he is married or that she is his student, patient, or employee—an interesting tactic because, ironically, it acknowledges the very forbidden zone that is already being invaded. At this point, it may seem ludicrous to imagine a man maintaining any illusion that he is not already explicitly propositioning the woman, although many men, if confronted, would still deny it.

How can a man touch a woman, touch himself, and make these comments without admitting that he has already crossed the line to overt sexual behavior? The answer lies in the power of sexual fantasy to intoxicate men so thoroughly that the distinction between inner and outer worlds becomes blurred. This erotic intoxication allows a man to live in two realities: one in which he is being sexually intrusive and another in which the normal professional persona can be trotted out at will for protection, disguise, and the maintenance in his own mind of a propriety that somewhere inside him he may wish to reclaim.

I think she's being seductive toward me. Some women do take the initiative in seducing the man, although most seductive behavior by women in the forbidden zone is a response to overt or covert provocation by men. When a woman begins a relationship of trust by being seductive, she demonstrates through her behavior the previous injury and cultural training that has instilled in her a self-destructive way of making herself important to a man. Under these circumstances, a man's responsibility not to allow sexual behavior between them is unmistakable. Yet restraint is more difficult for a man when a woman is being seductive—especially if he has been harboring a sexual fantasy about her.

When a woman behaves in an explicitly sexual manner within the forbidden zone in response to covert seduction, a man whose behavior is questioned will often deny he has acted provocatively, playing instead the role of the surprised innocent. The flaw in this innocence is that it is rarely accompanied by his refusal to accept the sexuality that the woman has offered him. Later, the man may maintain that he became sexually involved as a response to the woman's need. Through tortured logic, he may admit sexual involvement but claim that rejecting her sexual advances would have injured her self-esteem, so he was actually acting in her best interest by allowing sex to take place.

Sometimes men attempt to justify their sexual exploitation by invoking the darker side of the masculine myth of the feminine: the image of the powerfully vengeful woman who becomes evil and destructive if she does not get her way. They claim that they agreed to have sex because they feared the woman's anger if she were rejected.

While there do exist destructive women who try to coerce men into having sex or who falsely accuse men of sexual exploitation, this is still a minuscule problem compared with actual abuse by men of forbidden-zone relationships. It is extremely unlikely that a man who is innocent of sexual exploitation will be found guilty; the problem remains that even men who *are* guilty almost never have to answer for it.

I'm fantasizing about exactly how I will seduce her.   If covert seduction is unsuccessful, the next step for a man who is promoting his sexual scenario is to take a more actively seductive approach. A man can spend long hours in his fantasy world envisioning countless different ways in which the first moment of sexual contact with a woman will take place. But if he is not willing to let these scenarios remain in the fantasy world, they become the basis for elaborate, detailed plans of an actual seduction. A man may rehearse in his mind scores of variations of how sexual contact might come to pass, with each run-through adding more fuel to his fantasy.

His planning covers two central issues: mental preparation and the actual physical scenario. The mental preparation consists of rationalizations and self-deceptions that allow a man to override moral or ethical considerations that might discourage him from going ahead. A man planning an act of sexual exploitation often has his own inner conflict about going ahead with it. Very few of the men who violate the forbidden zone are cold, amoral people who could be labeled evil or sociopathic.

Instead, most men who sexually exploit women are in pivotal conflict between the life-giving and destructive sides of their own personalities. The next three steps a man passes through on his way toward an improper sexual liaison—the practical, emotional, and moral considerations—are less visible than many of the preceding steps, because they are part of a man's inner battle between the different sides of his personality.

Practical considerations: Can I get away with it?   The considerations here are strategic, not moral. The central question is "What will having this sexual liaison cost me?" in terms of money, prestige, professional status, disruption of marriage and family, relations with colleagues. Men often give short shrift to these practical considerations because they know that the chances are extremely small that a woman will mention an exploitative sexual relationship to anyone at all, much less to anyone who has disciplinary authority over a man in power. And in the unlikely event that the woman does lodge a complaint against him, as matters now stand he would most likely never be penalized.

Most women never speak out about exploitative sex, and those who do can encounter a nearly impossible uphill battle against public shame, the statute of limitations, burdens of proof, procedural and bureaucratic nightmares, and a masculine tendency toward mutual protection that discredits and blames women who bring such charges. The reality of the social environment is that men have until now been able to get away with sexual violations of the forbidden zone; on a practical level, sexual exploitation has been low-risk behavior.

Emotional considerations: Can something that feels so right be wrong?   Men also disregard risk for purely psychological reasons. When intoxicated by their sexual fantasies, they can easily develop magical feelings of power and invulnerability that cloud their judgment. When a man's involvement in the fantasy world has reached a certain stage, he may pass the point of no return. He feels either that he is untouchable by the outside world or that the sexual relationship he is seeking is so important that it is worth any risk.

Yet even at this advanced stage, most men retain, in some compartment of their psyches, elements of their personal integrity, morality, and professionalism. Men in power are usually talented professionals who have chosen to help others as their life work. Their willingness to abandon their demonstrated altruism is one of the tragedies of sex in the forbidden zone.

Sexual involvement with female protégées or other women who are sexually off-limits is not a special liability of the marginal, barely competent man. Success itself puts a man at higher risk for feeling that he can make his own rules and that his word (or his fabrications) will be believed against the word of a woman who challenges him. In most of the case histories I gathered for this book, the man who had a sexual relationship in the forbidden zone had been considered an outstanding member of his profession.

Some men who have sex in the forbidden zone have no need to create a moral justification for what they do. They go ahead on impulse, or simply on the feeling that they can get away with it. Other men creatively distort to their own advantage the basic agreement of relationships of trust: Because they know they must always act in the best interest of their protégées, it is both convenient and tempting to conclude that a sexual liaison with the object of one's fantasy is good for her.

When the man's involvement with his fantasy life is this far along, it is easy for him simply to decide that, for her own good, the woman really wants and needs to have a sexual relationship with him. There is no difference between this man rationalizing his action as being in the woman's best interest and a man who says, "She really wanted it," in response to a whole spectrum of sexual abuse ranging from mild harassment to outright rape. The point of view of a man's sexual fantasy world can completely take over defining the morality of his act.

As a practical tactic, men who come before disciplinary boards or courts on charges of sexual misconduct frequently argue eloquently, even persuasively, that they were acting in the woman's best interest. As an inner maneuver, reframing the woman's needs in this way removes the last rational obstacle a man may have restraining him from engaging in forbidden-zone sex.

The final moral consideration: the voice of the self. When there is nothing left to restrain him, the final barrier for a man who is close to consummating sex in the forbidden zone is his feeling that to go ahead would violate the deepest part of himself. Although someone who has gone this far has probably lost touch with it, the voice of the self sometimes breaks through to us just when we are on the brink of moral disaster. No matter how much effort a man has made preparing the ground for a forbidden sexual encounter, he still has the choice at any moment, with the support of his deeper self, to step back from such an act.

All restraint gone: the decision to move ahead. When a man has broken through the restraint of practical, emotional, and moral considerations, he is ready to give himself over to enacting his sexual fantasy. A man who is ready to act begins to feel the intoxication of timeless freedom and timeless danger that accompany sex in the forbidden zone. He has already crossed the boundary on his own. Now the only question is how he will bring the woman along with him.

Dual relationship: arranging a meeting outside the office. Out of a last, desperate hope of legitimizing the sexual relationship, a man may try to arrange a meeting with a woman away from the usual professional locale, such as in an out-of-the-way bar, restaurant, or motel. Because they recognize that sex cannot be part of their work together, they try to invent a parallel world in which they can have a simultaneous personal relationship.

This ploy relies on complete self-deception: When a professional relationship exists, it is psychologically impossible to have a truly separate, or "real," relationship that ignores the professional one. The forbidden zone is a condition of relationship, not a geographical happenstance. The degree of trust that a women has in a man, and the amount of power he has over her because of his emotional importance to her, do not disappear if they meet somewhere else.

Sometimes the proffered meeting away from the office is cloaked in respectability. For instance, a mentor might suggest that a protégée go to a lecture or seminar he is attending—it might even be one that he is giving himself. By meeting her outside the office, his fantasy-hope is that it will loosen the final restraints he feels on the expression of his sexual desires, which he hopes she will at last now have an opportunity to reciprocate. "Maybe we'll be talking to each other as people drift off afterward," the reverie may go. "Maybe one of us will suggest we have a drink or a cup of coffee. Maybe she'll need a lift home. Something is bound to bring us together."

Men sometimes find that the magical quality of forbidden sexuality is intensified if they can split sex off from the office or sanctuary, much as men who have mistresses tuck them away in apartments of their own, literally compartmentalized from the rest of their world.

When a splitting of locale occurs between the sexual and professional relationship, the outer charade of professionalism is sometimes abandoned, though at other times it may be kept up. A man might say to a woman, "We will have therapy in my office Tuesdays and Thursdays where you will discuss your problems. But we'll also meet in a motel to pursue our sexual relationship every Monday and Wednesday night."

As absurd as this sounds, men can become so identified with their fantasy worlds that they believe these fabrications. And the women they victimize, wounded and confused by the betrayal of their trust, are too paralyzed by fear and self-doubt to extricate themselves.

Do we talk about it first?   A purely logistical decision for a man, before he attempts to consummate his sexual fantasy, is whether or not to talk about it. Sometimes a man simply embraces the woman, deciding that he has her silent consent or that he needs no further permission from her.

If he does talk about it, he may be straightforward and matter-of-fact ("I want to go to bed with you"). Or he may exhort the woman to adopt the rationalizations he has already prepared to justify their sexual relationship ("This will bring us closer so that I can really help you"), still attempting to convince her that the sexual liaison will be for her own good. If she has not yet adopted this view through his psychological pressure, he will attempt to win her over through verbal persuasion.

Some men offer women their rationalizations but are fully prepared to have sex whether the woman involved agrees with him or not. Other men are so guilt-ridden and conflicted that they try to extract from the woman permission to exploit her. The man who goes ahead no matter what the woman says is so invasive that he really doesn't care what the woman thinks. The man who wants a woman's permission needs simultaneously to exploit her and to receive her absolution for his guilt about it. Neither of these scenarios leaves a woman any better off: They simply represent different styles of exploitation.

Many men at this point drop any pretense of rationalizing their impulses and become what, underneath the power and protection of the forbidden zone, they really are: ordinary men trying to win a woman's body in ordinary ways. They will often simply admit that they have been longing for the woman and explicitly proposition her.

No decent interval: terminating a forbidden-zone relationship in order to have sex. Some men who exploit women in forbidden-zone relationships, fully aware that sexual relating constitutes a serious ethical breach, simply declare a sudden end to the professional relationship and consider themselves completely free to pursue the woman involved as if no special relationship had ever existed.

This is often a dazzling, dramatic event that has an enormous impact on the woman involved. A man who has become important to her shows how important she has become to him by coming out from behind his professional role and declaring that he wants a personal intimacy with her. He promises her a relationship without forbidden-zone constraints, and he may even back it up by promising to sacrifice his marriage. This kind of declaration from a man has a powerful, nearly irresistible effect on a woman whose quest for specialness has never been fulfilled. And she is likely to agree to it.

The phrase "a decent interval" is used by therapists in an

attempt to identify an ethically acceptable way of turning a professional relationship into a personal one. Unfortunately, the interval between the termination of a professional relationship and the beginning of a sexual one is not usually determined by considerations of decency. Few men who are willing to change the rules of a forbidden-zone relationship in such a radical way are capable of supporting a state of mind that allows them to wait even a few hours before consummating their sexual fantasy.

The interval between the artificial end of the professional relationship and the beginning of the sexual one is often only a few minutes, and it is characterized by an intoxicating giddiness in the man, who anticipates his fantasy life finally becoming real. In this compressed, confusing time, a woman can scarcely collect her conflicting feelings enough to oppose the breakdown of the sexual boundary between them.

There are other problems with the notion of the decent interval. Time alone cannot change an exploitative relationship into a healthy one. Instead, underlying psychological factors determine whether such a relationship is damaging to a woman. Sexual exploitation of relationships of trust is so psychologically similar to a violation of the incest taboo that the rule against sexual intimacy arising from forbidden-zone relationships almost always should, as it does for father and daughter, last a lifetime.

The idea of the decent interval is useful if viewed not as a waiting period before going ahead with a sexual relationship but as a time for both people to collect themselves and question the meaning and necessity of such a step. Psychological intoxications tend to be episodic and time limited: If a man and woman who contemplate crossing the forbidden barrier stop seeing each other and seek consultation with other professionals, the chances are high that within a few months the fantasy will be sufficiently diluted, for one or both of them, to prevent it from being acted out.

For no matter what other feelings emerge between a man

and a woman in the forbidden zone, a sexually forbidden zone it remains. This is an emotional fact that is not subject to choice. As an emotional fact, it is as real as a physical fact, and no amount of wishing, choosing, or fantasizing will make the forbidden zone, and the responsibilities that attend it, disappear.

The act itself. The first sexual touching between man and woman in the forbidden zone may come with or without words, with or without warning, with or without any sign of agreement from the woman. For most of the women interviewed, the first overt sexual act was poignantly symbolic of the lack of caring that characterized the man's decision to have sex.

Barbara Forsch's psychiatrist, for instance, teased her for weeks with his covert seductiveness, then subjected her to his conflict and guilt over his attraction to her. When he decided to give in to the sexuality between them, it took the form of his insisting that she fellate him, despite the fact that she had explicitly told him in the "therapy" part of their relationship that this act was especially painful for her because of childhood molestation.

This type of experience exemplifies the reasons why sexual behavior in the forbidden zone almost always turns out to be unexciting and highly unsatisfactory. The sexual act itself makes clear the degree to which the man has already, on a psychological level, been using the woman as an impersonal object in his own inner world, and the woman consciously or unconsciously feels it. Almost all of the women I interviewed reported feelings similar to the woman who reported that she had been "treated like a piece of furniture" after she began a sexual relationship with her workplace mentor.

At first, the sex itself is more likely to be exciting for the man as part of his giving in to his magical inner fantasy. But the magic soon wears thin. After his sexual act, he has to begin facing the reality of the woman he is exploiting. Eventually it gets through to him that she is not really there to fulfill his sexual fantasies but is being compliant because of psychological coercion, rather than sexual desire. When he discovers this, he will feel cheated, as well as furious at the woman for his disappointment. He will resent the very compliance he has provoked. In retaliation, he may abruptly terminate their relationship, or berate the woman for her "sexual inadequacy" (i.e., her failure to live up to his fantasy).

When the masculine myth of the sexually healing feminine fails him, the man has great difficulty facing the real, wounded woman behind the myth. In her humanness, she forces him to face the truth that no magical solution to his pain is available. In her woundedness, she reminds him of his own denied injuries. It is no wonder that when men are finished with an exploitative sexual relationship, whether after a few minutes, months, or years, they often wish the woman they have exploited, who reminds them of how they have violated themselves, would simply disappear from their lives.

The aftermath: love and marriage in the forbidden zone.   The man who terminates a professional relationship with a woman so that they can begin or continue a sexual one is well on his way to the ultimate rationale of forbidden-zone sex: It is true love, and they have every right to pursue it. No matter what the rules say, real-life relationships do develop between older male mentors and their younger protégées. The number of marriages between men and women who met in forbidden-zone relationships is sometimes cited to defend the idea that such liaisons are not necessarily damaging.

Sadly, my research suggests that the odds against a healthy marriage evolving from forbidden-zone origins are almost insurmountable. Let me outline the tremendous obstacles involved. Even when both people initially feel that they are in love, because such feelings have developed under the special, protected conditions of the forbidden zone, they are almost always entirely the product of a healing fantasy rather than a true sense of who the other person really is. Months or years of self-examination are necessary to sort out how much of this love is actually for the other person, rather than for one's fantasy. Those who take the time to sort it out almost always discover that the love was for the healing, not the sexual, part of the relationship.

Such feelings of love, especially for the man, tend to wither when exposed to the light of normal life. If both people give themselves the time to sort out their feelings of forbidden-zone love, they may at best still care for each other, but rarely do they discover that they wish to be companions for life. At worst, the man quickly loses interest in the woman. And both of them have to face the fact that his claim of true love was spurious to begin with, either because it was a self-serving lie geared to sexual conquest or the product of a temporary intoxication. Unfortunately, this is the more frequent fate of apparent love when there is sexual contact in the forbidden zone.

My estimate is that well over 90 percent of "true love" declarations that grow out of forbidden-zone sexual relationships do not last longer than six months. One or both people clearly do not want to see the other again on a personal basis, and because they have crossed the sexual boundary they can no longer retrieve what may originally have been a valuable healing or mentor-protégée relationship.

But what of the few relationships with forbidden-zone origins that endure for more than a year, or that become marriages? Most of the ones that I have heard about simply perpetuate exploitative power dynamics into the marriage itself. If a woman could not protect herself from being exploited by a man when he was her therapist, pastor, or teacher, there is little reason to expect that she will be in a better position to protect herself when he is her husband.

Nevertheless, some readers of this book who are in long-term love relationships that had forbidden-zone origins may feel that they constitute an exception to my observation that most such relationships continue to be exploitative. I certainly do not want to remove hope that this could be possible, nor to judge the quality of intimacy between people I do not know. The hope is that you are right, that you have defeated the great odds against you and forged a relationship free of exploitation.

But this hope is accompanied by a warning and a plea: The warning is that, even when it is possible to transcend the inequality of power that existed when the relationship began, it is almost never done without both people looking very closely together at how they now handle power between them. The plea is to ask honestly whether there is an ongoing exploitative pattern in your relationship. If there is, it is never too late to try to change it.

THE POSITIVE SIDE OF MASCULINE PSYCHOLOGY: AMBIVALENCE AND HOLDING BACK

Now that we have traversed the stages through which a man sexualizes a forbidden-zone relationship, I want to balance this scenario by outlining the more caring and compassionate elements in men's psychology that restrain them from exploitative sexual relationships. Chapter 7, "A Guide for Men," builds upon these ideas with suggestions for practical steps men can take when they are feeling the sexual temptations of the forbidden zone.

The human psyche is complex, able to hold many contradictory feeling states simultaneously. Even a man who is easily intoxicated by his sexual fantasies has an innate ambivalence about acting them out. Some parts of him, if he can make contact with them, are free of this intoxication and aware that it is in his own interest, as well as the woman's, *not* to go ahead with a sexually exploitative act, even when the way is clear to do so. The following sections summarize the protective, empathic motivations that hold men back from sexual exploitation.

Holding back out of responsibility to protect the feminine.   When a man in power realizes that a woman under his care will not stop him if he wishes to have a sexual encounter with her, the most readily available reason to hold back is his sense of the responsibility that accompanies his power. Men who become healers, pastors, lawyers, and teachers may have complex and mixed motivations behind their choice of profession. Certainly, these men often behave in ways that invite their being caricatured as insensitive, lecherous, aggressive, power hungry, materialistic, and selfish. In this book I have even emphasized, in order to combat our denial, precisely the ways in which men in these professions act out these negative characteristics. But it is important to remember that each of these professions is, in pure form, a call to serve others. Although it may take some work for them to express it, these men of power are also motivated by their altruism, compassion for the wounded, and protective feelings toward the vulnerable.

Holding back out of moral choice.   Men also experience holding back from inappropriate sexual involvement out of a clear moral choice. "This is wrong," a man can tell himself, "for this place, for this time, for this woman, for myself." His moral and ethical stand can come from the values of his profession or from his personal religious or spiritual values. The more consciously he can acknowledge his ambivalence—the tension inside him between holding back and yielding to sexual involvement—the surer he will be that a resolution to his conflict can be brought about by his making a clear moral choice.

Holding back out of fear.   Sometimes a man holds back out of fear—not simply of being caught, but a fear of the psychological consequences, such as feelings of rejection, failure, or engulfment. Men may yearn for an intense connection to the feminine, but they also dread involvement. Despite its fascination and life-giving properties, sometimes the feminine is experienced as too all-powerful. The man feels like a young child in the presence of a mother. He doesn't want to get too close to this presence because he will feel so small, powerless, or dependent. Out of this fear evolves his healthier needs for autonomy, self-definition, and self-sufficiency.

Holding back out of service to inner masculine wisdom and strength. No matter how much a man measures his self-worth in terms of outer prestige, accomplishment, and recognition, he also answers to a private, inner standard of masculine value. Ultimately, a man wants to be able to live with himself. These inner standards are often pitched at a higher ethical and moral level than the culture demands of him. When a man resolves his sexual conflict in the direction of refraining from an exploitative liaison, he will be rewarded with an inner experience of wisdom and strength far beyond anything he could have anticipated. As a man orients himself to wisdom and inner strength, he finds that they offer him far more enduring value than brief sexual flings.

Holding back out of service to the inner feminine. A man's search for the inner feminine is a central piece of the complex puzzle of masculine sexuality. It is through the inner feminine that a man can finally feel that he has a source of life inside him. This inner source safely balances his motivation to exploit women, sexually or otherwise. He can begin to discover that, contrary to his original belief, a woman's body is not the only medium through which he can touch the source, the mystery, the ecstatic, the forbidden, the unexpected, the beautiful. There is another point of access to all of this, straight into a man's own nature, his own self.

From deep within, men are able to find feelings and experiences that explore the range of what our culture calls the feminine. For men who have been raised to meet the culture's collective standards of manhood, this range of qualities is often buried deep inside. They have been encouraged to turn away from these capabilities of the self, to look instead to the female body and psyche to supply them. But they reside inside as active, living structures that have evolved as men have taken in the experience of the feminine around them. For us as a species, there is probably survival value to have as wide a range as possible of flexible, creative response to different human situations. For a man this is expressed as the inner feminine; for the woman it is the inner masculine.

Men can be receptive as well as intrusive, cooperative as well as competitive, intuitive as well as structured, nurturing as well as consuming, compassionate as well as ambitious. This balance, when a man develops access to it, can save and enhance his life. It is especially important to bring an opposing, balancing force to bear on the destructive or self-destructive side of masculine psychology. Within the Western tradition this balancing energy is identified as feminine. Other cultures speak eloquently of these differing forces: The ancient Chinese concepts of yin and yang as described in the *I Ching* are particularly helpful examples, showing how wisdom dictates movement away from the extremes toward healthy, dynamic balance.

What we now call the feminine has always been with us as a special kind of relation to life and to the environment. It is oriented toward creation, not destruction, of life, and in harmony, continuity, relatedness, renewal through regeneration, and finding a place for everything in the whole that does not seek to destroy.

We need access to these values in order to prevent disasters of masculine imbalance. Such disasters take place on the personal level through such events as sexual exploitation; they take place on a wider level in the exploitation, rather than protection, of the natural environment; and on the global level in the threat of nuclear war.

A man squanders the opportunity his forbidden-zone sexual fantasies present him with when he takes the road that our culture has taught him and makes the irrevocable crossing of the forbidden boundary to touch the woman under his care. He becomes a victim of the fact that there are few barriers, except for those he creates for himself, to the rapid progression from preliminary erotic stirrings to sexually exploitative acts.

When men sexually exploit relationships of trust they do more than victimize the feminine; they trivialize and deprive themselves. When, instead, a man treats his fantasy life with the same restraint and respect he owes women, he can open himself to a true treasure trove of creativity, self-esteem, and inner aliveness.

6

A Guide for Women:
Guarding the Sexual Boundary

The next two chapters offer suggestions on how to translate the psychological complexities of forbidden-zone relationships into practical, health-directed acts. My hope is that women will also read the guide for men to learn more about what men can do to prevent sexual exploitation, and that men will also read the guide for women to gain empathy for the ways in which women struggle to establish sexual boundaries. Each chapter concludes with a section for women and men as parents, which identifies what parents can do to increase or decrease the likelihood that their children will participate in exploitative sexuality.

The guide for women focuses on the issue of boundaries. Although the suggestions contained therein are specific to forbidden-zone relationships, many of the boundary issues I discuss can be applied to all male-female relationships. When a woman ventures behind the closed doors of the forbidden zone with a man who has power over her, her ability to guard the sexual boundary will depend on how well she is able to *recognize, monitor, shape, and defend* it. Each of these steps will be addressed in psychological and practical detail, including suggestions for the prevention of future boundary incursions and for the difficult task of recovery for women who have been injured by past sexual-boundary violations.

RECOGNIZING THE BOUNDARY

Many women simply do not know that for a man to have a
sexual relationship with a woman when he has intimate
power over her life violates clearly established ethical, moral,
and legal guidelines. If a woman has experienced boundary
violations in childhood, she may be psychologically incapable
of even recognizing boundaries. Either because she was
brought up in a world where they did not exist or she was
sufficiently punished for trying to establish them, as an adult,
she has become conditioned by her fear not to think about
boundaries at all in sexual situations with men.

Other women have no problem with the general concept of
sexual boundaries and may even be highly competent when it
comes to helping other women. But even they can become
emotionally paralyzed (as described in chapter 4) when it
comes to establishing a sexual boundary, face-to-face, in a
forbidden-zone relationship with a man. A corporate lawyer
who for two years had sex with her physician during his office
hours related how she felt about it at the time:

> When my doctor first suggested we have sex, I saw nothing
> wrong with it. I thought it was a wonderful idea. Even when
> I was in law school I had trouble seeing what was wrong
> with it. It wasn't until I began assisting attorneys with sex-
> ual harassment cases that I realized how adapted I was to
> accepting whatever definition of sexual boundaries a man
> offered. That's why I think a lot of women don't put up any
> resistance when our boundaries are pushed in relationships
> where we shouldn't have to be worrying about defending
> them.

Whether they had never learned to recognize boundaries
or whether they blocked out their awareness under psychological pressure, more than half the women I interviewed were

not aware that it was a specific ethical violation for a man who was their therapist, pastor, teacher, or lawyer to have sex with them. Such women are at a terrible disadvantage if they have been denied this fundamental reality.

The ethical codes of most male-dominated professions clearly state that sexual relationships with people under their care are wrong. The codes of the four major professional groups that account for almost all psychotherapists—psychiatrists (M.D.'s); psychologists (Ph.D.'s); social workers (L.C.S.W.'s); and marriage, family, and child counselors (M.F.C.C.'s)—state much the same thing in their own way. The psychiatric code of ethics simply says, "Sexual activity with a patient is unethical." The psychologists say, "Sexual intimacies with clients are unethical." Social workers state, "The social worker should under no circumstances engage in sexual activities with clients." The marriage counselors, in view of their family orientation, extend the range of prohibition somewhat when they say, "It is considered unethical to have sexual relations with one's clients and/or client's spouse/partner." The different psychotherapy professions have either established or are now formulating additional ethical codes which state that sexual relations with *former* clients and patients are also unethical.

In addition, because violations of these ethical principles are so catastrophic for clients, several states have passed legislation making it a *criminal act,* and in some cases a *felony,* for a therapist to have sex with a client. Many other states are in the process of enacting stronger civil and criminal laws against sexual abuse by therapists and pastoral counselors.

All of the major religious organizations consider sexual relations between a pastor and parishioner to be highly unethical. Nevertheless, for a variety of reasons there are fewer clear statements to this effect from the clergy. For one, there are so many different religious groups, each with a tradition of complete autonomy, that it is difficult for them to join together in a consensual ethical statement.

Religious organizations also have a desire to handle their ethical problems far away from the public eye and are not obligated to reveal their ethical codes and disciplinary procedures. And most religious groups do not like to draw attention to the fact that sexual misconduct by their clergy even takes place, so they are not motivated toward generating public statements concerning this problem.

Many religious groups hold sexual activity between clergy and parishioners to be so overridingly wrong or sinful that they have never felt it necessary to say so. Consider, for instance, the Catholic church or any other order in which the priesthood is celibate. If one has taken an oath not to have sexual relations of any kind, it may be seen as superfluous to specify that a clergyman must not have sex with a parishioner. As one priest told me, "The church's position seems to be that since we can't do it at all, there is no point in telling us *with whom* we can't do it."

The legal profession is, like the clergy, fragmented and somewhat indirect in its approach to the issue of sex between lawyer and client. Each jurisdiction (state or federal) has its own ethical code, so it is difficult for them to speak with unanimity about ethical issues. In addition, many laws that relate to ethical conduct are addressed by court opinions on a case-by-case basis, rather than by a broad-based rule. Lawyer-client sex, if it can be proven in court, will almost always be considered unethical, negligent, and damaging to the client because it violates *other* ethical precepts. Sex with a client is almost universally considered to be a *breach of fiduciary duty* (the duty to act at all times in the best interest of the client), as well as a violation of the lawyer's obligation to provide representation without *conflict of interest*. But with public concern about ethical issues increasing, there is now a growing movement in the legal profession to adopt a uniform, clear statement that sex between lawyers and clients is, as the lawyers would put it, *per se* (in itself) unethical.

The ban on sex between teachers and students is covered

by overriding laws against statutory rape until the student is eighteen years old. In colleges and universities, there is a growing movement to recognize through clear ethical guidelines the sexual and emotional vulnerability of the student to the unequal power of the professor. Many leading universities have adopted policies that make it specifically unethical for faculty members to have sexual relationships with their students, even when both have allegedly consented to do so. Here is what the University of Iowa has to say on the subject:

No faculty member shall have an amorous relationship (consensual or otherwise) with a student who is enrolled in a course being taught by the faculty member or whose academic work (including work as a teaching assistant) is being supervised by the faculty member.

Faculty members exercise power over students, whether in giving them praise or criticism, evaluating them, making recommendations for their further studies or their future employment, or conferring any other benefits on them. Amorous relationships between faculty members and students are wrong when the faculty member has professional responsibility for the student. Such situations greatly increase the chances that the faculty member will abuse his or her power and sexually exploit the student. Voluntary consent by the student in such a relationship is suspect, given the fundamentally asymmetric nature of the relationship.

Because it questions the whole validity of consent in relationships of unequal power, the Iowa policy could serve as a model for many other forbidden-zone relationships, including sex in the workplace.

Unfortunately, the workplace offers no such sensitively written ethical guidelines to address sex between mentor and protégée. Although the power inequality is present, the other element that defines the sexual forbidden zone—trust—is not usually considered to be a requirement of workplace relationships. Laws against sexual harassment in the workplace address a woman's right to be treated with decency and respect, free from abuses of power. These laws continue to develop in ways that protect women from sexual injury, but they do not yet address relationships of trust in which a woman may have offered her consent to having sex with a boss or mentor based on the less visible, psychologically based power dynamics of the forbidden zone.

Nevertheless, in the workplace and in many areas of life that do not fall under a discernible ethical code, forbidden-zone conditions of unequal power and the need to trust still exist, making sex a damaging violation of the woman's selfhood. Until businesses can address these issues institutionally, the ethical standard must come from each individual, out of respect for himself, herself, and the other.

MONITORING THE BOUNDARY

The all-important act of recognizing that forbidden-zone sexual boundaries really exist opens the way for the next step: learning how to monitor the boundary. This means being able to see where the boundary is and what is being done to it at any given time in the development of a relationship.

The sexual boundary is very easy to see once one has accepted its existence. At the moment of acceptance, it is as if a special light has gone on that illuminates previously invisible particles and projectiles crashing into a thin, flexible barrier. What is maddeningly unfair is that men, whenever they are around women, see this boundary with a compelling clarity, which is one way that they exert their power. A man locates the sexual boundary between himself and a woman with an instinctual ease. Then, if he wishes, he can play with the boundary as if it were the net in an especially interesting tennis game. In this game, each of his words, gestures, and fantasies is an intended step toward that net.

Once a woman is committed to seeing the boundary, she will find her own metaphor, her own sense with which to perceive it. Then she can begin to see how the previously described feminine dynamics of the forbidden zone operate for her. She should then be able to see with a new clarity how men use the masculine dynamics to push beyond appropriate boundaries.

Although some aspects of the boundary depend on plain intuition, many indicators are easily visible. For instance, does the man in power gradually or suddenly approach you more closely, or touch you in any way? Does he change the time or frequency of your meetings in a way that might lead to greater intimacy? Does he speak words that seem to be overly personal or that have a sexual tinge? This is not to suggest that *any* drawing closer or development of intimacy is wrong or dangerous—it may be perfectly innocent, or else part of the development of nonsexual intimacy that can allow a forbidden-zone relationship to realize its fullest potential of hope and immeasurable value.

The point is that all such activity at the boundary of intimacy is *highly significant.* It must be noticed and recognized as possibly the most important dimension in the entire relationship. The more a woman monitors the boundary, the better basis she will have for judging whether a man's behavior toward her is respectful or injurious.

Critical information about what is happening at the boundary of intimacy is not easily visible through the five senses but can be monitored instead through one's intuition and feeling. Many women know from instinct and inner feelings when something in a relationship with a man is wrong. Such feelings can be physical; several women remarked that they experienced nausea, muscle tension, or trembling as their first perception that a man was improperly sexualizing a relationship. Or else the feelings can be psychological—a sense of dread, anxiety, depression, or blackness that comes on when she is with a man, or a few hours after seeing him.

Sometimes a woman will feel nothing more than a free-floating suspicion, or inner *knowing,* that something is wrong. Too often her response to this kind of perception is to try hard to be reasonable about it, and if she can't find a piece of outer reality to support it, to set aside the messages.

It is extremely dangerous to dismiss the validity of boundary information received through feeling and intuition. While they are not infallible, such perceptions are likely to contain a wealth of important and accurate information about events that are not yet visible. They are like an early warning system. Intuition and feeling reach directly into the deeper psychological dynamics that determine so much about what happens at the boundaries of intimacy between a man and a woman. Through this medium it is possible for a woman to see what is happening in a man's inner world of sexual fantasy *before* he challenges the sexual boundary.

Of course, a man is entitled to his sexual fantasies and should not be condemned simply for having them. Even if a woman is right about sensing a man's developing fantasy involvement with her, there is no certainty that he will act with any impropriety. On the other hand, there is no certainty that he will not, and a naive belief that a man has no desire for sexual involvement in the forbidden zone helps pave the way for exploitation. A woman, in her recognition of the man's possible sexual agenda, is mentally preparing herself to reclaim the power to guard the sexual boundary.

SHAPING THE BOUNDARY

The all-important question is what to do with both the sensory and intuitive information received from monitoring the sexual boundary. How does one become active, rather than just a passive observer, in the task of determining how a man will relate to a woman in the forbidden zone? Many women need no coaching at all in acknowledging and monitoring the boundary of intimacy. Yet they remain paralyzed at the level of *action,* of participating with men in power who are used to acting alone in shaping the boundary of intimacy with women.

I believe that nearly every woman who is ready to work at it can act with equal power to men in determining how they will treat her at the sexual boundary. But the key word is *work.* Changing old patterns is hard work, and it takes time.

One reason it is so difficult to change the power dynamics of sexual boundaries is that any woman who takes on the task has to confront not only her personal history but centuries of cultural history that have granted men power over the boundary. Another reason is that the human psyche produces significant changes only with the full involvement of its deepest parts. It takes time to reach down, past the layers of behavior that we have learned in response to past injury or to social necessity, and live more and more with the integrity of the self, of who we really are.

But it *can* be done, and while you can't get there today, you can start today. No matter how trapped one feels, the smallest step toward doing something different begins to generate hope that bigger changes can come, and the psyche thrives on this hope. Moreover, when a woman begins to generate her own fantasy of hope from inside, she is starting to weaken one of the central dynamics of sexual exploitation: the projection of the fantasy of hope onto the man.

Talking about Boundaries:
Taking the First Step

One small step a woman can take today is simply to start talking. Talk about boundaries, about what it feels like to be in a closed room with a man who has power over you. Start talking about sexuality—how you feel it coming toward you from men, what it stirs inside you.

Talk to other women—friends, sisters, coworkers, supervisors, aunts, mothers, grandmothers, daughters. You will quickly discover that nearly every one of them also feels the tensions of sexual-boundary issues with men. You will give one another permission to uncover and begin speaking about incident after incident of sexual-boundary problems. For some women, the boundary issues will be puzzling and ambiguous—mysterious, interesting, and disturbing all at the same time. They will have felt both the excitement of the sexual tension and, even if they can identify no specific way it has injured them, also a degree of unease, threat, or fear.

Many other women also will be able to tell you of a specific incident in which forbidden-zone sexuality was overtly expressed. They will tell you how they became sexually involved with a man who was their therapist, doctor, clergyman, teacher, or mentor. Or they will tell you how a man in one of these positions cast a sexual nuance on their relationship, throwing the woman into terrible conflict and forever compromising the original purpose of their relationship. They may even dare to begin remembering a long-suppressed incident of sexual molestation from childhood. As more women ·feel support for revealing these secrets, we will discover that the incidence of childhood sexual-boundary invasions in women is more extensive than we can now imagine.

Talk to men. If approached, it is altogether possible that a friend, brother, father, or husband will tell you something about what it feels like to be on his side of the sexual boundary and how he perceives his role with women. He doesn't have to see this situation as you do, and he doesn't have to take your side. Perhaps he will say some things that disturb you because they confirm the enormous differences between the ways men and women approach the sexual boundary. As long as he is reasonably respectful of your asking, shows some willingness to talk about the way he sees things, and listens to what concerns you about sex and power, you have begun a process of bringing these issues out of the silent world where very little can change.

You might also talk to a man with whom you now have a forbidden-zone relationship. For a woman in the forbidden zone, talking actually *shapes* the boundary. If the man has been respectful of boundaries, he may be receptive to talking with you about how he sees things, and you will learn something from him. If there is already a sexual undercurrent in the relationship, talking tends to defuse it by bringing the tension into both people's awareness. When a man begins to develop a fantasy of forbidden sex, he may be torn between keeping it concealed in his secret world and wishing to defuse the fantasy, which he may recognize as being destructive to his and his protégée's well-being.

Given a man's ambivalence about participating in forbidden sex, the very act of a woman bringing up boundary issues provides him an opportunity to relate to her reality instead of his fantasy world. When he hears a woman talking about sexual-boundary issues, he can no longer believe that she knows nothing about boundaries or is afraid to participate in shaping them.

A cautionary note when talking to a man about sexual boundaries: He may interpret your interest in boundaries as evidence that you are flirting with him, as an indication that you may want to sexualize the relationship. To guard against misinterpretation, you must be as clear as possible about why you are asking. For instance, you might say something like, "I understand that sexual tensions sometimes enter relationships like ours. I'm bringing this up because I certainly wouldn't want sexuality to interfere with our working relationship."

In this way you are shaping the boundary simply by letting it be known that you are aware that these issues exist. Even if the conversation does not go much further, you will have made a strong impact by demonstrating that you already know about and are actively involved in monitoring the boundary between you.

Talk to a therapist, counselor, or pastor, male or female— either someone you are already seeing or someone you seek out to begin examining sexual-boundary issues. Despite the abuses of power that occur in the helping professions, the majority of practitioners are both competent and ethical.

Many women who have been sexually victimized, either in the forbidden zone or by molestation as children, cannot bring themselves to reveal the secret of their sexual victimization even to therapists they have worked with for years. For these women, breaking the code of secrecy is an enormous achievement, opening the way for release of a torrent of feelings and memories that have long been hidden out of guilt, shame, and fear. Talking in this way begins to restore a protective boundary within which healing can take place.

Talk to a women's support group, even if there may be other individuals with whom you can already talk about sexual-boundary issues; it will provide a different sort of help. Women have been isolated from one another as sexual victims, and restoring a sense of feminine community is vital not only to the recovery of individuals but to the rebalancing of masculine and feminine values in the culture. A women's therapy group, or simply a women's discussion group without any therapeutic agenda, would be a good place to start.

Alcoholics Anonymous (AA), Al-Anon, or Adult Children of Alcoholics groups are highly recommended. They now exist in almost any community, and usually some women-only groups are offered. Because substance abuse blurs boundaries both inside and outside the individual, the psychological dynamics of chemical dependency bear many similarities to those of sexual-boundary violations, and the two are often intertwined. Some communities may have specialized groups for sexual victims—such as rape and incest survivors—as well as Women Who Love Too Much groups (based on Robin Norwood's book of the same name).

Talk to a woman you believe is being victimized. Many women who have trouble shaping their own boundaries are still able to respond empathically to other women in pain. If you see a woman around you—friend, family member, co-worker—who appears to be a sexual victim, try to talk to her about it. The connection you make with her may ultimately bring both of you out of silence into an active, shaping role in relation to men and sexual boundaries.

DEFENDING THE BOUNDARY

It is a gift to women when men do not force them to defend the sexual boundary. But women cannot afford to remain passive and merely hope that the appropriate boundaries will be maintained. As soon as a woman feels the specialness of connection that permeates forbidden-zone relationships, she must also realize that the man can incorporate that specialness into his sexual fantasies.

Because of this, women are continually at risk for experiencing sexual-boundary pressures from men, whether at work, in the family, on dates, or in the intimate atmosphere of the forbidden zone. Women who have not yet felt this pressure are almost certainly likely to, and as we have seen, a hidden multitude of women have already suffered from major boundary invasions. At fatal moments their culturally induced passivity has been exploited by men who have chosen to play out their own sexual fantasies. If this violation is to stop, women must take the ultimate step of learning how to assert control over the sexual boundary. Beyond recognizing, monitoring, and shaping, they must learn how to actively defend—and if necessary fight with all their strength—against these incursions.

A woman can defend her boundaries whether she is recovering from violation that has already taken place, putting a stop to one occurring in the present, or preventing one from happening in the future. It can be done through inner work and outer action. It can be done alone, in groups, or in direct confrontation with the man involved. Most important is to make a small beginning step. With each small step you will help break apart the underlying psychological patterns that lock women into positions of exploitation. As you chip away at the underlying patterns, you will gather strength, from yourself and from others. And your strength increases with each step you take.

Defending the Boundary Face-to-Face

The full power of the hidden psychological pact that forces women to collaborate in their own exploitation asserts itself when a woman is right there in the room with a man who may be abusing his power over her. Although it is particularly difficult for a woman to begin defending herself face-to-face, in challenging the man's power up close she may be able to draw on inner reserves she has never before used.

If a man introduces sexuality, by innuendo or physical gesture, where it does not belong, a woman must immediately act or speak in response. If she does not, her silence encourages him to continue eroding the sexual boundary.

If she wishes to act immediately and is prepared to risk losing the relationship, she can simply get up and walk out of the room, never to return. This is the purest possible statement of noncollaboration with sexual-boundary pressure. Although it removes the chance for negotiation of the boundary between them and leaves the woman open to having possibly misjudged the man, surprisingly large numbers of women interviewed felt in retrospect that this is exactly the step they wished they had taken.

Although the suggestion to leave the room puts the most extreme solution first, it is important for a woman to establish for herself the right to do so at any time, even when she is trying to work on the boundary issue by talking to the man about it. Part of the psychological trap that keeps a woman in the room with an exploitative man is her propensity to feel that she somehow owes him more than simply walking out, that she might hurt him, that she might be wrong about him. A woman in a forbidden-zone relationship with a man does not owe him any of this.

If she is correctly reading his behavior as being sexually inappropriate, she has handled the situation correctly by leaving. If she is wrong about him, it is not her job any more than it is his to correct the mistake. If the man has been misunderstood, there is nothing to prevent him from trying to express his point of view or asking her to explain her precipitous behavior.

Sometimes a woman, given time to think over what has happened or to talk it over with a friend or therapist, may conclude that she has acted unfairly. Under these circumstances she can apologize to the man involved and ask that he understand her suspiciousness about these issues. A man with sensitivity toward women's boundary issues might be able to accept her apology, possibly even resulting in a deepening of the nonsexual aspect of their relationship.

Nevertheless, it is preferable for a woman to leave a relationship too soon rather than too late. Sometimes it is difficult to determine with certainty whether sexually inappropriate behavior has taken place or is being threatened. Rather than become a victim of the need for certainty—which often comes only *after* an abusive act has taken place—a woman who leaves too soon at least creates safety for herself during the time it may take to consider what actually occurred.

I say this knowing that a woman has a lot to lose if she simply walks out on a man who has power over her future economically, psychologically, physically, or spiritually. But in her freedom to make this sacrifice, if need be, a woman breaks the hold of masculine power over both her body and her sense of self, even if it involves a period of painful deprivation. As she understands what she has gained through enduring, and mourning, the loss of relationship to the man, she will, especially with support through therapy or a peer group of women, be in a better position to come back to the outside world with her own self-defined strength, along with an insistence that she be treated with respect.

There are, however, many other situations in which a woman may experience some sexual-boundary tension but is not in a position to sacrifice a relationship of value with the man, or else feels she has more to gain by staying and discussing what is going on between them. If she begins with the simple, direct statement "We need to keep sexuality out of here," she must then closely monitor his response. If he seems surprised and denies everything, she can say, "Fine. Maybe I was wrong. But whether I was right or wrong, I'm sure you'll agree that sexuality has no place in the relationship between us." If he offers a seductive response, such as "Why not?" she can leave, or else simply reassert, "Because sexuality is not what I want, and it just doesn't belong here."

It may seem unlikely that a healthy professional relationship could continue after interchanges like this. In a therapy or pastoral relationship, the trust has already been breached by the innuendo alone, and it is probably impossible to go on. But in the workplace or with teachers and lawyers, the man may be able to recover his sense of boundaries after having tested them. Although you should never have had to deal with it, once you established that you are not going to be involved, many men will drop the subject and go on with the work you were supposed to do together. Of course, if a man continues to act sexually despite your clear statement that it doesn't belong, you may have no choice but to leave.

Confronting Your Ambivalence

My suggestions are based on the fact that sexuality is a *betrayal* of the forbidden zone, not on the assumption that a woman does not to some degree *wish for* sexual contact with a man in these relationships. Women as well as men can be highly ambivalent about having sex in the forbidden zone, because the healing hopes we project often express themselves through sexual images. A woman's ability to accept her own forbidden sexual feelings and fantasies will actually help her deal with them. It is important for her to confront and accept her sexual desire, if she has any, and not let it undermine her knowledge that sex in these relationships is destructive.

A woman has the same right to her sexual fantasies and desires as does a man. They can provide her with a gateway to her inner world, and they need to be respected as such. Guilt in a woman about her forbidden sexual fantasies must not rob her of her ability to say no at any point. Even if she has been overtly seductive—as were several of the women whose stories have been presented here—she has the right to turn away from sexuality the moment she can assert control over her boundaries. Although men in relationships of trust have an ethical or legal duty to refuse sexual contact even when it is offered, the sooner a woman stops participating, the less she collaborates in the damage he may cause her.

Dealing with a Man's Anger

One of the forces that is most likely to paralyze a woman when she tries to challenge a man's incursion on the sexual boundary is her fear of his anger. Unfortunately, this fear is often justified. Men who want to maintain full control over the sexual boundary can become angry if their control is challenged, so a woman must be prepared for this. A man's anger may take one of several forms:

- He can continue to deny that he did anything sexual, throw the issue back at you, and make you feel guilty for accusing him. If he does this, you must fight your guilt and leave the relationship.
- He can simply dismiss you and terminate the relation-

ship. In effect, he has brought about what would have happened if you had walked out of the room, except that you will be less prepared for this sudden termination. The psychological challenge to a woman in this situation is to understand that it is better to bear the pain of mourning this unexpected loss than to have silently tolerated his boundary incursion.

• He might try to coerce you to stay with him by playing upon your guilt and feelings of unworthiness, or by threatening you with retaliation if you leave him or reveal his sexual behavior. This is the classic psychological trap that a victim of childhood incest or sexual molestation finds herself in. Sadly, the power dynamics of many relationships between adults create the same dynamics as these abusive childhood experiences, which bind women to their oppressors.

You might not be able to leave this kind of relationship right away, but you *must* find someone sympathetic and start talking about it, resolving to leave this man as soon as you have the strength to do so. You must risk his anger at your leaving him; at least you will have a chance of protecting yourself from him at a distance. As long as you stay, you are certain to be abused.

• Finally, he could both dismiss you and threaten to retaliate. If he does this, you will probably have to act at the next level of defending the boundary—not up close, but from a distance, using legal and ethical sanctions.

Defending the Boundary from a Distance: Filing an Ethical or Legal Complaint

The legal system has a somewhat well-deserved reputation for unresponsiveness to women's complaints of sexual exploitation by men. Most women would rather absorb their injury privately than risk the ordeal of a public battle in which they are likely to become targets for deeply held "blame-the-victim" attitudes so prevalent in our culture.

Yet the realm of official ethical and legal complaint is a vast, virtually untapped resource for women in terms of its potential to offer both justice and healing for sexual wrongs. The law may seem in many ways rigid and static, but it is not. It is actually quite fluid and responsive to evolving social forces. In both legislatures and courts of law, momentous alterations are taking place in our society's ability to recognize and remedy specific injuries to women arising from inequalities of power.

In light of this, women hold in their own voices powerful instruments of change. Each public complaint of abuse of power, sexual or otherwise, helps undo the secret pact that allows men to believe that women will be available to fulfill their exploitative sexual fantasies, and then silently absorb the injury. A significant healing of the fundamental injury to women occurs whenever a woman raises her voice merely to *ask* for justice, whether or not justice results (although if competently pursued, a growing number of official actions against men are successful). Each voiced complaint undoes millennia of denial of sexual injury to women and lends increased credibility to the complaint of the next woman. Given this potential, for women to continue feeling shut off from the legal system would represent an enormous tragedy, an ongoing concession to the messages that have silenced them up till now.

Moreover, filing an official complaint is not always an ordeal, nor is it as public as one might expect. Many different channels are available, once a woman gives herself permission and begins looking around. Many women have found, to their surprise, that men as well as women can respond supportively and empathically to complaints of sexual impropriety. Although opportunities differ from state to state, certain guidelines exist on how to begin lodging an official complaint. The options fall into the categories of ethical, administrative, civil, and criminal action. *Note*: None of the following information should be construed as legal advice; it is wise to consult an attorney before filing any sort of complaint.

Ethical complaints.   These are usually handled privately and confidentially, offering a woman a somewhat protected environment for voicing her grievance. Ethical complaints can and should be made to any organization, public or private, with which a professional has an affiliation. Any professional who is employed must answer to the ethical standards of the organization that employs him, and complaints can be directed to his employer as well.

Although most doctors, lawyers, and therapists are self-employed, they usually maintain professional affiliations with associations that have ethical standards. For instance, psychotherapists usually belong to a professional association consisting of other therapists with their professional credentials (e.g., American Psychiatric Association; American Psychological Association; National Association of Social Workers; state or national associations of marriage and family counselors). Many therapists and doctors also teach, and any college or university they are affiliated with can receive an ethical complaint.

Doctors belong to county and state medical societies or to groups based on their specialties; most doctors have privileges at hospitals, and all hospitals have committees to hear ethical complaints about any doctor on its staff. Lawyers belong to local or state bar associations. Pastors are overseen by the ethical standards of the religious denomination to which they belong. Professors and teachers must answer to ethical and sexual discrimination procedures of their own schools.

Most applicable professional organizations are listed in the Resources section of this book. These organizations should be able to direct you to a branch in your area.

Whenever a woman has experienced a sexual-boundary violation from a man in a professional setting, she should find out which organizations he is affiliated with and lodge an ethical complaint. This will consist of putting down in writing the facts about what occurred. In doing so, a woman begins to establish the reality of the boundary violation and to send a message that its occurrence cannot simply be wished away. Stating the facts is all that is required, although the facts can certainly include both the external and psychological impact the violation has had on the woman. Although it is usually up to the ethics committee to determine the punishment, a woman may also suggest an appropriate redress from the man involved, whether it is a formal apology or the return of fees paid.

Ethics committees will, upon receipt of a complaint, usually ask the member complained about to submit a statement or to meet with them to offer his version of events. The woman who complains may be asked to appear before the committee to present information or answer questions. If the member presents a credible story in which he denies any unethical behavior, and if the committee sees no obvious evidence supporting the charge (such as statements by third parties), the committee has no power to ascertain what occurred and may do nothing. If there are holes in his story, or if he admits to some level of unethical behavior, the committee can take action ranging from a warning through probation, suspension, or expulsion from its organization. It can ask, as terms of probation or suspension, that the member make some restitution to the complainant, engage in community service, and/or undergo counseling. If a member does not cooperate with an ethics investigation, an ethics committee has no power beyond expelling him from membership, nor does it have power to award financial damages.

There is much to be gained from an ethics investigation even if it does not result in any significant punishment to the man. It establishes a record in case there are other ethical complaints about the same person. Many men who sexually exploit professional relationships are so-called repeaters who count on the silence of their victims. As women speak out, men will no longer have the protection of silence and will be more likely to incur punishment if they cannot restrain their acting out.

Administrative complaints.   Doctors, therapists, and lawyers all practice under licenses granted by state licensing boards. Although there is variation from state to state, these boards have the power to hear ethical complaints and, if necessary, to impose discipline on a professional ranging from a warning to a revocation of his license to practice.

Agencies that license doctors and therapists go by a wide variety of names and are usually located in state capitals. The state bar is the agency that licenses lawyers. Most telephone directories have state government listings that give numbers for information about how to direct a complaint. If this does not work, ask for help from the local office of the state legislator who represents your district.

Administrative hearings by state licensing boards lie somewhere in between the closed, private atmosphere of ethics committees and the public exposure of courtrooms. As with an ethical complaint, a woman should describe the facts of what occurred and the damage she suffered as a result. The board will then ask the professional for his side of the story. Some licensing boards have budgets allotted to conduct their own investigations and are not limited simply to choosing which story to believe. If they receive several unproved complaints against the same person, they can send out undercover agents to gather direct evidence of a professional's sexual misconduct.

Procedures usually remain confidential unless the board decides to impose discipline on the licensee, in which case it becomes part of the public record. There is wide variation from state to state in the degree to which the identity of the woman complaining becomes public knowledge. Of course, the person complained against has the right to know who has lodged the complaint.

Many women lodge complaints to a state licensing board to protect *other* women from unethical sexual behavior, even when it is too late, because of the statute of limitations, to receive justice in court for themselves. (There is usually no time limitation for either ethics committee or licensing board complaints.) It can take a woman many, many years to recover enough from a sexual-boundary violation to give her injury public voice. But statutes of limitation usually limit lawsuits to anywhere from one to five years from the date of the injury. It took several of the women interviewed for this book ten or twenty years to come to terms with the reality of their injuries, far too late to sue. But when they realized that the same man who injured them might be damaging other women, they finally broke their silence by making complaints to state licensing boards.

A professional is permitted to have an attorney represent him in an administrative hearing. Many such actions are resolved by a stipulated (negotiated) agreement. In order to expedite a resolution, the licensing board may allow the professional to bargain for a temporary suspension of his license or for probation, without admitting wrongdoing, and on the condition that the entire proceeding be kept out of the public record. At other times a professional will agree to a voluntary surrender of his license in return for dropping all charges. The licensing board makes the decision whether to accept a stipulated decision, not the person filing the complaint. While stipulated decisions involve some concession by the professional, an agreement to keep the matter confidential helps maintain the secretive atmosphere in which sexual-boundary violations thrive.

Nevertheless, the more voices raised to ethics committees and licensing boards, the more the reality of sex in the forbidden zone will be revealed. As with ethics committees, licensing boards may at times not have enough evidence to take any action, but they will keep the complaint in their records to be available if future complaints are lodged against the same man. In addition, a woman who brings ethical charges on these levels still retains her right to sue in a court of law, as long as her action comes within the statute of limitations.

Civil complaints.   Courts of law have become an important arena for the raising of the feminine voice. Women who have been victimized are often represented in court by female attorneys. Of course male attorneys are often thoroughly competent, committed, and impassioned in defense of female clients, but in terms of the recovery of the feminine voice, there is incomparable symbolic value for a woman to be guided through the intricacies of the legal system by another woman.

Civil action for sexual misconduct by a professional man can be brought against the man himself and, under certain circumstances, against agencies he was working for in his professional role, such as clinics, hospitals, governments, churches, universities. If a woman has complained to an ethics committee, a hospital board, a university sexual-harassment committee, or a state regulatory board, action can be taken against any of these bodies if they are negligent in the way they have handled her complaint. This option becomes important when an institution such as a school, hospital, or religious group tries to cover up an incident and does not give the woman a fair hearing.

Women who complain and who are fearful of having to relive their painful trauma are easily pressured into dropping their action in return for token punishment to the man. The woman may be asked to maintain silence about the incident and to agree not to pursue the matter further before a licensing board or in court. Such agreements, however, can be challenged in court as being coercive and as further exploiting the woman in her injured state.

In a civil action, a woman can request both compensation for her actual injuries and extra compensation for punitive damages. Such actions, when successful, result in the occasional six-figure or seven-figure awards that make headlines. But most lawsuits never come to trial. Their success or failure rests on the skill with which an attorney pursues the action through the complexity of complaints, pleadings, investigations, briefs, motions, depositions, discoveries, and settlement conferences in which most of the art of the law takes place.

The legal process can at times quickly bring a woman a sense of recognition of her injury, as well as a monetary settlement. But it also can last years and threaten to preoccupy and exhaust both her and her attorney. Nevertheless, if handled correctly, pursuing legal action can become a healing journey regardless of the final monetary award. Therefore, for both legal and psychological reasons, the central task is to find the right lawyer. He or she should be someone who not only believes that your case has legal merit but also understands that there is a psychological dimension involved that is more important than financial or legal victory; there should be a willingness, as well, to listen occasionally to how you feel about pursuing the case.

Although it is not essential to hire a female attorney, more and more women lawyers are specializing in civil suits based on sexual harassment and misconduct, and they may have the most experience and competence in handling these cases. If you have no direct way of finding such a lawyer, call or write to one of the organizations listed in the Resources section of this book.

Because statutes of limitations vary from one to five years (depending on the state and the specific grounds of the lawsuit), a woman should contact an attorney as soon as she has any inkling of ever wanting to file a lawsuit. Even if a woman remains ambivalent about whether to take this course (as is so often the case), in some instances an attorney can help her preserve her rights without committing herself to a lawsuit. Some lawsuits can be filed with the court under seal in order to come under the statute of limitations, leaving the option of either pursuing or dropping the action at a later date.

Criminal complaints.   Some violations of sexual boundaries, in or out of the forbidden zone, may fit the legal definitions of rape, sexual assault, or battery. Essentially, rape is defined as sexual intercourse in the absence of consent, although charges can also be brought for other sexual acts performed without consent. District attorneys who decide whether to prosecute criminal cases may not recognize the psychological inability to give consent that is usually present in forbidden-zone relationships, and they usually require evidence of physical force. A civil attorney can be engaged to help frame a complaint properly to the police and the district attorney, and at times a woman can sue a sexual assailant for civil damages even if he is neither brought to trial nor convicted on the criminal charge.

In Minnesota, Wisconsin, and Colorado, therapist-patient sexual contact is by law a felony, which is a serious criminal act. Several other state legislatures, including those in California, Massachusetts, New York, and Ohio, are in the process of considering legislation either to make it a criminal offense or to strengthen the civil code to make it easier to sue for these acts. If a professional is found to have violated ethical guidelines, licensing regulations, or criminal statutes, this can also be used as evidence against him when filing a civil suit.

WHY CAN'T I FIGHT BACK?
A SUMMARY OF PSYCHOLOGICAL TRAPS

Although the way is open to a broad variety of means by which women can recognize, monitor, shape, and defend the sexual boundary, strong psychological forces continue to prevent women from fighting back against sexual exploitation. The most prevalent of these internal traps and conditions follow, along with suggestions on how they may be worked through.

A victim's state of mind.   Your own seductiveness, apparent consent, or level of sexual arousal makes you no less of a victim than if you didn't have those feelings. In the forbidden zone, the man in power holds a trust to maintain the barrier against sexual contact, no matter what the provocation. Female sexual victims have already developed patterns, in response to familial and cultural demands, of being seductive, agreeing to what a man in power wants from them, and smoothing over conflicts by being compliant in the moment. Sexual arousal can occur even under conditions of forcible rape, and its presence in no way diminishes the man's sexual abuse.

Self-blame.   Take responsibility for your part in a sexual-boundary problem, but do not take an unfair share of it. For every overresponsible woman there is a man who does not take nearly enough responsibility for his inappropriate expressions of sexuality. Some women believe that because they apparently consented to having sex in the forbidden zone, they are equally responsible. This ignores both the hidden power dynamics of relationships of trust and the man's specific responsibility to not allow sexual contact. A woman needs to take responsibility not for the sexual violation itself but for understanding the mix of personal, social, and familial dynamics that led to her victimization.

Hopelessness.   Do not believe people who tell you that it is not worth trying to fight victimization. It may appear at times that the mountain of pain you have to face by looking at the issue, either privately in therapy or publicly by filing a complaint, is insurmountable. But once you make the first

step, you begin to gather strength from unseen inner resources, and you place yourself in a position to get help from
other people.

Inability to ask for help.   "I should be able to handle this
myself" is a message many victims repeat to themselves. But
nobody has firm, healthy boundaries about matters of intimacy unless somewhere along the way—in infancy, childhood, or adulthood—she had the help of someone who modeled healthy boundaries and taught her how to shape and
defend her own boundaries of intimacy. If a woman wants to
escape a pattern of repetitive boundary violations, she cannot
do it by herself. She needs the same help—from friends, former victims, therapists, attorneys—that anyone who now
knows how to create healthy boundaries has at some time
been given.

Compassion for the man.   Do not attempt premature for-
giveness or reconciliation. Many women are so anxious to put
a sexual-boundary violation behind them that at the slightest
show of contrition they prematurely forgive or reconcile with
the man who has injured them. This gesture, together with
overresponsibility, are disguised ways of continuing to nurture the man's injury.

    Take your time to understand, in depth, the meaning of
what the man did to you and what it means that you allowed
it. Although it is possible to reconcile, forgive, and put the
experience behind you, with or without official complaints,
somewhere along the line a woman probably needs to become
deeply angry at the man for what he has done, even if the
anger is never visibly expressed.

GETTING ANGRY

Taking any of the steps outlined in this chapter constitutes, to
some degree, an implicit expression of anger. The ability to
experience anger at being victimized is a critical factor in a

woman's recovery. I have sat with victims and witnessed them becoming visibly angrier, by the minute or hour, as we spoke. Painful as this stage may be, it is inspiring and hopeful, not primarily because it means she might fight back against the injustice that was done to her, but because of what it means for her own sense of self.

Patricia Elmont, the psychologist whose sexual relationship with Dr. Thomas Stuben was described in chapter 4, offers us an example of the recovery of a sense of self that often accompanies becoming angry. Years after her sexual relationship with Dr. Stuben ended, Patricia began therapy again, this time with a woman. Finally offered an authentic healing experience, she was able to realize her inner potential in what she considers to be a specifically feminine way. She describes her anger at realizing how much sexual-boundary violation she used to tolerate:

I think women have to deal with this problem in all of our lives—defending our boundaries and not even knowing when invasion is happening, not knowing how to say no, not knowing we have a right to question. There is anger built in once you see the system and how excluded the feminine is, despite the power and strength of female values. Once the scales began to fall from my eyes, I was angry at every man, and the whole system.

Nevertheless, Patricia retains a hopeful vision for mutual respect between men and women:

It's hard for men to stand their own masculine ground and just honor or adore the feminine. The man who is overwhelmed by it needs to subjugate and enslave it. And sometimes it's hard, but a woman can stand in a fully female place and just adore masculinity. That could be wonderful, but we're not there yet.

There is a fascinating epilogue to Patricia's story that provoked her into what she called a "powerful blast of rage." After
not hearing from him for twenty years, Patricia received an
inquiry from Dr. Stuben, asking her to evaluate, for his research, her therapy with him. Her reply follows:

Thomas,

That you would write me without mention of our past
sexual involvement implies to me that you have no sense
of the gross violation of ethics you committed nor any
sense of the gross violation of my person it was. I am
sickened and disgusted by what you allowed to happen,
by your apparent ignorance of the transference—or
worse, your conscious exploitation of the transference.
You seemed to feed off dependent women. I and who
knows how many others became members of your own
private brothel, and what you offered in the name of
therapy and healing you turned into greedy, self-serving
gratification.
      You did not have the imagination to see who I was.
You had no idea what was forming in me and no
sensibility of holding the boundaries in order for that
fledgling to emerge. You lack the ability to contain
sexual energy for the work of healing and development,
and therefore act out and kill any possibility of
transformation. What you allowed to happen with me is
despicable. I am furious that I did not take you to court.
You are a prey on women, an embarrassment, and a
menace in the profession.

Patricia

      Patricia's story is important because it illustrates the in-
verse ratio between a sexual victim's self-punitive feelings and
the ability to get angry at what has been done to her. As she

punishes herself less, she is able to mobilize her anger more, which in turn makes her even less self-punitive. And even if she never takes external steps to redress the wrong done to her, the recovery of anger not only heals her self-hate but expresses her growing conviction that she deserves better.

Many sexual victims have been taught, early in life, to believe that they deserve whatever kind of ill treatment they happen to receive, either because that is the best that the world has to offer or because of family messages that say their worthlessness makes being victimized a just punishment. Recovering the right to be angry, and to express it or not in any way she wishes, helps a woman ensure that she will go back out to the world with a feeling of deserving to be treated respectfully and having her gifts honored. There is nothing more hopeful than this for achieving satisfying relationships in or out of the forbidden zone.

A GUIDE FOR WOMEN AS PARENTS

Mothers and Sons

Rather than describe any particular behavioral strategy for mothers toward their sons, I would instead like to emphasize that the work women do to value themselves—not allowing themselves to be abused, healing their suffering, and raising their own voices against victimization of themselves and other women—will be felt by their sons of whatever age. As women begin to take steps against their own victimization, it changes their sons' attitudes toward women and sends a message of hope to their children's generation that the cycle of abuse can be interrupted.

The degree of self-respect a mother has as she is raising her son will be a major determinant of his attitude toward women. Because the mother-son relationship takes place at such a primal level, his mother's inner sense of herself has a key effect throughout childhood on a boy's ability to respect and value the feminine.

This factor combines with many others—such as his father's relationship to women, cultural messages from role models, peers, and the media, his experience of the girls and women he meets—to shape a boy's feeling for the feminine. Yet he will, knowingly or not, continue to refer back to the matrix of femininity that was provided to him early on and that is also constantly being updated by his mother.

No child can be exempt from the emotional impact of parents who are themselves injured, deprived, and in turmoil. In fact, a child who knows something about his own parents' pain—as long as he sees that they are not overwhelmed but are able to model constructive ways of working on it—will be equipped to develop healthy ways of dealing with the inevitable losses that life from time to time brings.

The critical point for any parent to remember is that it is never too late to begin working against destructive feelings or behavior—whether manifested by depression, addiction, permitting or causing abuse of others, or by sexual exploitation. If you start taking the smallest step today, it will eventually have a healing impact on you and on everyone close to you—especially your children of any age.

Mothers and Daughters

The mother-daughter relationship is the most important one of all in determining whether a girl will grow up knowing how to deal in a healthy way with masculine power. Her relationship with her father may create the more visible patterns of how she relates to men, but the bond with the mother will shape her deepest sense of self.

As is true of the mother-son relationship, any psychological work a mother does in revaluing herself as a woman will have a strong effect on her daughter of any age. Although men can remain centrally important in her life, the critical work for a woman—mother or daughter—is to develop a feminine sense of self-esteem that does not depend on the judgment or permission of men.

A mother must do more than stop collaborating in abusive relationships with men; she must turn toward her daughter and tell her as much as possible about uniquely feminine experience, so that as her daughter grows up she will feel her heritage as a woman. This means talking to a daughter, from infancy on, in positive terms about her body—how it looks outside, what it conceals inside, what changes it will undergo, how it contains the mystery of life.

As a daughter goes through the critical developmental stages of puberty and the beginning of menstruation, a mother can tell her what these experiences were like for her and impart feminine lore that may reach back through the generations. As her daughter grows, a mother can increasingly share with her the complexity of feeling states, the psychological and spiritual dimensions of being a woman.

Because so much exploitative behavior toward women as children and adults involves sexual or physical abuse of their bodies, the orientation of a mother toward this kind of intimate valuing of her daughter's body is of the utmost importance in imbuing a natural sense of privacy, boundaries, and inviolability. This will not prevent men from trying to encroach on her boundaries, but it will do much to ensure that she does not collaborate in degrading and abusive treatment.

Of course, the values that a mother imparts verbally about her daughter's role toward men and her right to pursue her ambitions in the outside world will influence that child enormously. But if a daughter knows from her mother that her body is a sacred container of the feminine spirit, she will have a lifelong treasure that can never be taken from her.

7

A Guide for Men:
Facing the Feminine in New Ways

Sexual exploitation of relationships of trust is a social problem that must be resolved psychologically, from the inside out, as well as culturally, from the outside in. External controls will not work until men and women recognize the inner factors that force them to repeat this mutually destructive drama.

No matter how well a man has prepared himself— through his education, training, and experience—for the moment when the sexual magic across the forbidden boundary exerts its alluring call, his ability to resist temptation arises only from his capacity to recognize the harm it will bring to the woman, and ultimately to himself, if he goes ahead. This inner struggle, if it is resolved by turning away from exploitative sex, allows a man to rediscover and heal his own wounds, instead of continually asking the woman to minister to him. Once a man recovers his compassion, he has opened the gateway to regaining the lost dimensions of his own self that he had been searching for in his fantasies of forbidden sexuality.

He will be able to understand his sexual fantasies as elements of his inner world, discovering their meaning and overcoming his shame. This in turn will enhance the possibility that some of the highly intimate contact with the feminine that he experiences in his fantasy life can actually be attained with a real woman, in mutuality rather than in exploitation.

As he does the work of looking inwardly, a man comes back to the outer world with new resources with which to face the feminine. He will begin to resent as an affront to his own integrity the protective schemes men build in order to maintain their sexual privileges. He will feel betrayed by, rather than admiring of, the father figures who support the devaluation of the feminine, for he will know that he, too, is being demeaned. His affiliation with values of equality rather than hierarchy will allow him to see women as colleagues and equals, rather than as objects of exploitation. And he will be able to defy the messages that encourage him to remain silent when he knows that people of any gender are being victimized.

A man's ability to work actively to prevent other men from exploiting women is especially important because not all men are eager or able to stop violating women's sexual boundaries on their own. Some men have no capacity to contact their compassion, even when given every chance. Such men, with an indifference to the pain of others that is the hallmark of sociopathy, will repeat their exploitative behavior as many times as they are given the opportunity. Their capacity for compassion for others was wounded so early in life that it can never be recovered, and they can be stopped from exploiting others only by external constraints. But it will take the efforts of men who *can* feel compassion to work together to restrain the men who cannot.

The following steps are offered as a guide to how men can work in psychologically and socially constructive ways when faced with the problem of sex in the forbidden zone. Although there is some variation from profession to profession in how a man should deal with his feelings, the suggestions that follow have been formulated so that they address the sexual-boundary issues that are similar in all mentoring and helping relationships between men in power and the women they are serving. *Note*: None of these suggestions constitute legal advice. Any man involved in potentially unethical or illegal conduct should consult an attorney.

The final section of this guide addresses the role of men as parents. It contains a summary of the destructive messages men give their daughters and sons about sexuality, as well as suggestions for addressing sexual dynamics in healthier ways.

Women who read this guide for men should gain a clearer picture of the work a man needs to do to prevent sexual exploitation. They should therefore be less likely to try to do that work for men or to become their victims. Women will also learn more about the standards of behavior they have a right to expect from men who are feeling the sexual tensions of the forbidden zone.

IF YOU'RE ON THE EDGE:
STOP AND GET HELP

When a man is on the edge of violating the forbidden boundary, he has a crucial, twofold task. His obligation does not end with the struggle, as difficult as it may be, to refrain from sexual enactment of his fantasies. He also must fight to maintain the original trust placed in him, to safeguard the elements of the woman's destiny that have been placed in his care.

In the long run, the injury of greatest consequence to a woman when a man crosses the forbidden boundary may not be from the sexual invasion itself but from her irretrievable loss of the purpose and meaning of their special relationship. The purpose may have been to foster her spiritual, professional, or intellectual development; it may have been to help her recover from injury, whether physical, emotional, or economic; it may have been a liberating rite of passage for her, which would have allowed her to pursue her career or find some measure of personal and social freedom. Whichever it might have been, the man on the edge still has a chance not only to spare a woman another destructive act of sexual invasion but also to strengthen the deeper purpose of the relationship.

This is the challenge to a man on the edge: First, he must refrain from any sexual action. Second, he must be sure that his sexual fantasies no longer skew his responses toward the woman. In short, he must give up all future hope of acting sexually with her. Third (and this can come only after the previous two requirements have been fulfilled), he must, when he is with her, set his sexual needs aside so that he can return to giving her the best that his professional role demands.

Finally, if he continues to be so overcome by his nonprofessional feelings toward her that he cannot maintain the highest standard of professional behavior, he must end their relationship with extreme care. In doing so he must clearly communicate to her that she is not to blame for this ending, that he is not angrily holding her responsible for the ending, that the ending comes out of respect for her rather than as another message that no powerful relationship with a man can exist without sexual exploitation. (This option will be investigated more fully later in this chapter.)

In accomplishing all of this against his onrushing erotic fantasies, a man certainly needs help. His decision to look for help, and the quality of the help he gets, may have a pivotal effect on his life and future, as well as on the future of the woman whose trust he must uphold.

By help, I mean finding someone with whom to talk. It can be a man or woman; a professional, such as a pastor or therapist; a colleague, brother, friend, teacher, sister, mentor, even spouse. The social role does not matter; what does matter is the attitude of the helping person toward the man on the edge, and the sensitivities the conversations help engender in him.

It is a hopeful sign when men can ask for help. Besides making them less likely to damage women, they are expressing a nascent awareness that they, too, have been damaged by our culture's distorted views of the feminine. In addition, a forbidden-zone crisis presents a man with a special opportunity to heal the loss of intimacy from the father, if as a result he can develop a new therapeutic or mentoring relationship with a man who is willing to share his own struggles with forbidden sexuality.

No matter to whom he turns for help, a man on the edge must be respected for having chosen to deal with a problem of his erotic fantasy life. The last thing he needs is a reaction of judgment that will make him even more ashamed of his inner life than he already has been. The more his inner experience can be valued, the better he will be able to perform the vital task of separating inner experience from outer act.

Conversations with the helping person also must direct the man toward understanding the great potential damage to the woman. To the extent that his struggle to maintain the sexual boundary helps him feel compassion for the wounded feminine, a man will have returned from the edge with a life-saving gift—not only for the woman whose trust he has preserved but for himself. With the right kind of help, a man can examine in greater detail the following four major requirements of successfully pulling back from the edge.

Not acting sexually. Although your task does not end here, it begins here. This is the fundamental step, without which the nonsexual value of the forbidden zone will be irretrievably lost for both of you. You must draw on any possible resources in order *not* to act sexually, even if they only get you through another day. No matter what you feel, *stay in your chair,* and make sure the woman stays in hers.

If no other form of restraint is working for you, you can try two extreme measures in an emergency. An emergency is the feeling that today is the day that you will not stop yourself from having sexual contact with your protégée. The first step is to cancel your next meeting with her, without explanation if need be. At this point, do nothing more than tell her, over the telephone, that something has come up in your personal life that makes you temporarily unable to see her.

If you can restore the professional boundaries soon, and if you have successfully concealed your sexual intoxication from her, you need never let her know. You have done her the favor of not involving her in your struggle to maintain the sexual boundary. But if you cannot safely restore your own boundaries, then phone and explain to her that you are referring her to another professional. How much to tell her about why you are doing this is addressed below in the section on terminating a forbidden-zone relationship.

The other emergency measure you can take, if you are actually with the woman in a session, is to *tell* her, in words instead of actions, that you are feeling that you can no longer respect the professional prohibition against sexual contact. While this involves her in helping you maintain your boundaries, at least you both will have a chance to deal openly with the problem. A man may be surprised to discover that his protégée can be of help in keeping the sexual boundary. Once a man directly states his sexual desire, instead of indirectly manipulating a woman because of it, he gives the woman an opportunity to tell him whether or not she wants sexual involvement—and in most cases he will discover that she does not. Even if she says she does, he must not permit it.

Relinquishing the woman as a potential sexual partner.   In addition to not acting sexually toward a woman in a relationship of trust, a man must finally relinquish her as a potential sexual partner. Women can have destructive and degrading forbidden-zone experiences with men who never touch them. Instead, these men hold the professional relationship hostage to their sexual fantasies. They never act out the fantasy, but instead of fostering her own self-respect and growth, they subtly undermine her self-esteem.

If the woman never responds to the man's secret sexual attraction toward her, he may covertly punish her for this by withholding his support for her. If he is a psychotherapist or spiritual leader, he can ignore or denigrate qualities in her that might develop her autonomy. If he is a mentor at work, he can stand in the way of a deserved promotion. If he is a professor, he can deny her the academic approval upon which her future depends. The abuse of power by men whose sexual fantasies have been frustrated is a phenomenon that causes extensive damage to women.

A man must relinquish the possibility that he will ever have sexual *contact* with a woman if he is to restore the trust of the forbidden zone. He need not give up his sexual *fantasy*; in fact, he should be encouraged to pursue that fantasy to its source, which is deep inside himself. But he must accept that the woman in his fantasy is *not* the one sitting across from him, and he must do everything possible not to turn the one into the other.

Relinquishing also includes giving up hope that the sexual contact will happen upon *termination* of the professional relationship. A sexual liaison that takes place after a merely technical termination of the professional relationship remains subject to the identical psychological dynamics of the forbidden zone, and it is identically exploitative.

A man should try to emerge from his forbidden-zone crisis with the strength to continue his relationship with a woman in a nonsexual way. This outcome protects a woman from the injury of being abandoned and offers both of them a hopeful message about the containment and healing of destructive expressions of sexuality. When a man's only solution to his crisis lies in disappearing from a woman's life, it reinforces the woman's belief that she will inevitably bear the brunt of men's difficulty in maintaining healthy sexual boundaries.

For many women, losing an important relationship because of unmanageable sexual tension repeats a pattern in which fathers abandon their adolescent daughters. Many fathers are warm, present, supportive, and loving to their daughters when they are younger, only to become angry, critical, demanding, and distant when faced with their daughters' sexual development. Filled with shame because of the presence of incestuous feelings and fantasies toward their daughters, many men distance themselves, depriving their daughters of healthy, nonsexual intimacy. Although this solution is far preferable to one in which a father acts seductively or incestuously, she still loses him.

Terminating a relationship of trust.   If termination of a forbidden-zone relationship becomes necessary, it is important to think about doing it in a way that injures the woman the least. If a man finds that the only way to pull back from the edge is to sacrifice the relationship itself, everything rests in how he explains this to her.

He will harm her the most if he simply avoids her and terminates their relationship without an explanation, or if he leads her to believe that the relationship is ending because of an inadequacy on her part. Either of these events would repeat the same hopeless litany: She will feel that, on the surface, the man abandoned her because he found her lacking in potential, competence, or intelligence. Underneath this, invading her awareness, will be the realization that he left her because she failed to cater to him emotionally or sexually.

A man must explain why he is ending the relationship without drawing the woman into his personal struggle by revealing too much. Ironically, in his sensitivity to this difficult task, rather than blaming her, a man has the chance to provide the woman an opportunity for healing by truthfully telling her that he is ending the relationship because he cannot properly uphold the professional boundary.

In a healing relationship he must offer to help her find another professional. If he is a professor or workplace superior, his obligation is to create a new situation for her: finding her a new academic mentor, or having her transferred to a different company department, on terms *she* thinks are fair. She will feel respected by this honesty and concern. She will still suffer a loss, but if she is left with a feeling that, in the midst of his sexual crisis, her feelings mattered enough for him to make some effort to spare her further damage, she may be able to go on to the next relationship of trust with a glimmer of hope where none existed before.

If a man contacts a woman in order to initiate a sexual affair *after* the termination of the professional relationship, he will be destroying whatever feeling he might have given her that the termination was out of concern for her. He has demonstrated that he never truly relinquished her as a sexual partner.

IF YOU HAVE VIOLATED THE FORBIDDEN ZONE: HOW TO MAKE AMENDS

If you are already involved.   Once you have crossed over the forbidden boundary and developed a sexual relationship with a female patient, client, parishioner, student, or protégée, the original helping relationship has been forever compromised and cannot be restored. The first step in trying to heal what has been damaged is to acknowledge that the professional relationship is finished and to curtail any attempts to carry on a dual relationship that includes sexual intimacy.

On the other hand, it is equally impossible to treat your relationship simply as a personal one, without addressing its forbidden-zone origins. Whether you intend to continue or extricate yourself from the relationship, you both must try to deal with the wound caused by your betrayal of your protégée's trust. Both of you should seek help in dealing with this wound. In addition to seeking therapy, you might ask the ethics committee of your profession for guidance. Ethics committees can sometimes arrange a mediated solution that can head off a painful, polarizing legal battle.

To make amends with the woman involved, you owe her an apology and your recognition that in allowing a sexual relationship to take place you have caused her harm. You may also need to make her an offer of restitution on terms *she* thinks are fair, subject to mediation if her demands seem inappropriate. When a man who has violated a woman's trust demonstrates that he understands how this may have affected her, he is giving her hope for the future.

She may still ask for financial restitution, which may have to be negotiated with a malpractice insurer in cases in which legal action for professional negligence is possible. If there is some justification for her seeking financial compensation, you can try to negotiate a fair settlement as part of the emotional repair, instead of opposing her and forcing her into a protracted legal battle.

If there is an incident buried in your past.   If there is no ongoing contact between you and the woman involved, you still might consider letting her know that you regret the incident and realize the damage it may have caused her. This should only be done in writing—never by a phone call. You must be completely nonintrusive in the way you contact her, leaving it up to her whether she wants to reply to or even acknowledge your gesture.

It is very important not to involve the woman in absolving you, forgiving you, or making it any easier for you to work through the consequences of your ethical violation. All of that is *your* job, and you will do it better away from her, preferably with some professional guidance. A man has to be careful not to repeat, in the attempt to make amends, the original request for the woman to heal him.

If there is no nonintrusive way available to give a woman a message that you regret a previous ethical violation, do not contact her. Instead, direct your efforts toward changing exploitative tendencies you might still notice in yourself or in the men around you.

Men and women with unresolved forbidden-zone incidents in their past often continue to see one another, at a distance, as members of the same extended community—at church, school, work, or through a network of colleagues in the legal, medical, or psychotherapeutic professions. Do not underestimate the degree to which old unhealed wounds continue to undermine the integrity of both people. Their affiliation in the community should provide them a way to resolve this injury, although the man must still be nonintrusive and respect the woman's right, if she wishes, not to take it up with him.

IF YOU HAVE NOT VIOLATED THE FORBIDDEN ZONE: BE HONEST WITH YOURSELF

Men do not attain positions of power and trust in relation to women by accident. They have invited this trust by choosing a profession that they know will bring them into intimate contact with women. Even men who conduct themselves according to the highest ethical standards of their professions can admit that underlying erotic fantasies may have played a part in their choice. They must realize that the inherent conditions of the forbidden zone place them at risk of feeling erotically intoxicated by the women they serve.

Being honest with yourself means simply this: Do not hide from the fact that something in your own nature has led you into having intimate contact with women in the forbidden zone. Do not be surprised when erotic intoxication strikes. Look to your own nature, not to the woman in front of you, to find the meaning and the way to handle your sexual fantasies. The more you acknowledge what is inside, the better prepared you will be to find the help you need when you need it, to avoid betraying the trust placed in you.

The following guidelines can help men prevent sexual exploitation of the forbidden zone and create an atmosphere that discourages exploitation by colleagues:

Acknowledge the importance of your fantasy. A man's forbidden-zone sexual fantasies create an opportunity for reconciliation with his own inner self. How a man regards his inner sexual stirrings, and whether he can begin to recognize his own voice within them, will lay the groundwork for a healthy response when his fantasies may press for enactment.

Know the wrongness of sexual abuse of trust.   No matter how tempted you may feel by the magical lure of forbidden sexuality, nothing makes it right—not even the woman's willingness to have a sexual relationship, not even her outright seduction.

Know the damage done to women.   A woman who engages in sex in the forbidden zone, whether she says she is consenting or not, is repeating a hopeless cycle of abuse that she has been subjected to most of her life. Each further episode of betrayal leaves her more cut off from the inner feminine voice and creates additional self-hate. Any further incident of sexual abuse may be the one that causes the death of hope itself, resulting in her becoming a permanent victim, or even in her suicide.

Help your colleagues.   The man who is honest with himself about his risk of sexual exploitation can be an important resource to other men. The more a man is willing to think and talk about the sexual undercurrents within his profession, instead of keeping men's tribal secrets that support destructive behavior, the more he can serve as a model to his students, colleagues, and sons.

Work to uphold and rewrite laws and ethical codes. There is little consistency among different professions and governmental jurisdictions in laws and ethical codes that address sexual exploitation. Some provisions could not be improved upon: They directly state that any sexual contact with a person one has met in a professional context is unethical and illegal. But in some professions and in the workplace, there are few clearly stated ethical standards that address forbidden-zone relationships. This may be because sexual exploitation is still officially denied. Some religious denominations find themselves in a bind about enacting official provisions against sexual exploitation, because the very act of discussing such a provision constitutes acknowledgment that sexual exploitation might exist among that denomination's clergy. Religious organizations, with their crucial moral authority, could make an important contribution to raising consciousness about sexual boundaries by making clear, oft-repeated statements about the unethical nature of sexual relationships with clergy.

Silent bystanders no longer—join others in speaking out. As Elie Wiesel observes in the quotation at the beginning of this book, the silence of the bystander allows victimization to continue. Ethical male professionals must realize that they have a pivotal role in letting their unethical colleagues know that sexual abuse of trust will no longer be tolerated. As long as it does not violate the wishes of the victim, all professionals should be required by ethical and legal codes to report any instance of sexual abuse they hear about to professional ethics committees for further investigation. When men commit themselves to breaking the silence that imprisons the victim and protects the victimizer, they will be sending a message of hope that an age-old collaboration in mutual destructiveness can finally be healed.

A GUIDE FOR MEN AS PARENTS

Fathers and Daughters

The father-daughter relationship is the childhood pattern that a woman most directly reexperiences when she enters a relationship of trust with a powerful man. How she will respond .

to sexual issues that may arise between them depends a great deal on what she learned about sexual boundaries in her relationship with her father. The rest of this section explores the various unhealthy and healthy ways that fathers influence their daughters' competence in setting appropriate sexual boundaries.

The father who oversteps his boundaries outside the family but tries to impose strict sexual boundaries on his daughter splits his view of the feminine, oversexualizing women outside the home and desexualizing his daughter (and often his wife). This pattern, which creates a double standard, often has disastrous consequences for daughters.

If her father has been too repressive, his daughter may become so afraid of her sexuality that she will disown it and lose her capacity for expressing it. But she is also at high risk for teenage or adult promiscuity because of her need to reassert control over her sexuality, often in angry, impulsive ways that do not distinguish between healthy and unhealthy liaisons. She may rebel by sneaking out of the house to have a sexual relationship with a peer or older man who, whether he exploits her or not, at least recognizes her sexuality.

Another pattern involves a girl adapting to her father's wishes when she is still living at home, without either losing her sexual capacity or becoming promiscuously rebellious. But if she has accepted the myth that control over her sexuality resides not in herself but in her father, when she leaves the family home she will be at high risk for yielding control of the sexual boundary to a male authority figure—perhaps a professor, pastor, or therapist. A father's successful control over his teenage daughter's sexuality may be a prescription for her later involvement in sex in the forbidden zone.

The father who is sexually invasive or who promotes his daughter as a sexual object does not have to be directly and criminally incestuous in order to train his daughter to feel that she must be sexually available to men. He might repeatedly touch her in overfamiliar ways that both of them accept as the norm. He may make comments about her emerging sexuality with a mixture of angry accusation and leering suggestiveness. He may make these suggestive comments in front of a guest in the house, or else may leave her alone with another man, inviting molestation. This father is so involved with his incestuous wishes that he is willing to sacrifice his daughter to another man so he can vicariously fulfill these fantasies.

The girls of these sorts of fathers become sexual victims within their families and almost always repeat their victimization when they leave home. As adults, if they find their way to relationships of trust with therapists, pastors, or other men in power, they are likely to behave seductively because they cannot believe that a man will give them attention for anything other than their sexuality. Women who have been encouraged to act seductively pose a difficult challenge to men in helping professions. These women are ready to play their part in the man's forbidden sexual fantasies. But if the man in power can resist the seduction and not permit the woman to repeat this destructive pattern, he can provide her with a singular, life-changing, healing experience.

A father can also be physically absent, or even if present can completely disregard his daughter's sexuality. The daughter of this father will feel deprived of self-esteem about matters far beyond sexuality. Her competence, intelligence, compassion, capacity for intimacy, and ability to define herself in the outside world may all remain undeveloped if her father, through physical or emotional absence, fails to recognize who she is.

This is a common pattern in women who become involved in sex in the forbidden zone. To make up for the lack of support by her father, the deprived woman seeks it, on virtually any terms, from a powerful man who offers her a semblance of special recognition. If a sexual relationship is the price of their connection, she will grant it to him.

In the case of the wounded father, some men keep their wounds carefully hidden, expressing them to their daughters indirectly through abuses of power, inappropriate seductiveness, or emotional unavailability. Other men exhibit their wounds clearly and directly—through alcoholism and other addictions, physical illness, depression and self-hate, violence, or the failure to deal successfully with work and with intimacy. Paradoxically, a father who manifests his wounds visibly can cause his daughter less damage than the man who hides them. Although the daughter forms a bond with her father's wound and in some ways begins taking care of him from an early age, a father with visible wounds may be able to acknowledge the importance to him of his daughter's love. If he does not exploit her love by either demeaning, controlling, or invading her, a wounded father who openly acknowledges the healing value of his relationship with his daughter helps her value herself.

But the fate of the daughter of a wounded father hangs in a precarious balance. She may instead become repeatedly involved in trying to heal men's wounds, unable to leave a relationship with a man even if his wound causes him to abuse her. Given this pattern, she may find it difficult to refuse the request of an authority figure who wishes to have sex with her, in or out of the forbidden zone.

Despite the obvious liability to a woman of having a bond with her father's wound, many female victims are ultimately (and usually through therapy) able to heal themselves by drawing upon a deep, previously unrealized source of strength that they developed as children tending to those wounds. And although many of these fathers end up destroying themselves or their families—through alcoholism, suicide, abandonment, or violent behavior—if a woman can discover that beneath these ruins her father truly loved her and considered her special, she has a chance to redeem this long-buried love as her own newfound strength.

Helping Daughters Develop Healthy Sexual Boundaries

A father who wants his daughter to develop healthy sexual boundaries will not be overly repressive, seductively invasive, or emotionally absent. He will doubtless manifest some wounds to his children, but a critical distinction that separates good from bad parenting is not the magnitude of the parent's wounds but the degree to which one is willing to take responsibility for them. For a father, this means that no matter what his problems may be with sexual boundaries elsewhere, he will make an effort to avoid turning his own daughter into a victim.

The biggest gift he can give his daughter is his own effort to come to terms with his wounds and the meaning of his forbidden sexual fantasies. He has a right to do this in complete privacy, seeking whatever kind of help he needs without her ever knowing the precise nature and content of his struggle.

To the extent that he can protect her from his unresolved wounds by working on them himself—whether they are manifested as substance abuse, depression, or in sexual-boundary problems—he will not use his daughter's emerging sexuality to punish her or to gratify himself. Instead, she may be graced by his interest in her world, his respect for her privacy and boundaries, and his encouragement for her to use her own strength inside and outside of the home.

Show interest in her experience. Children learn early on how much room there is for them to express their individuality in the family and in the world. If they are not listened to, they will believe that their feelings and ideas have no importance. A father who does not want his daughter to turn into a victim will take time to listen to her and to show interest in how she sees things. One-to-one conversation, as opposed to lecturing and disciplining, is a priceless gift for a child, no matter what her age. A father need spend just a few minutes a week doing nothing else but conversing with his daughter, asking about her world, telling her in response a little about his childhood and, as she grows up, about his adult world. If this continues week after week, year after year, she will know that who she is matters to the world, and she will be less willing as an adult to accept a relationship in which her own feelings and ideas do not matter to the other person.

Show respect for her privacy and her boundaries. Children have usually developed a clear sense of boundaries between themselves and others by the time they are three, when they are able to exercise control over the boundary both physically and verbally. From as early an age as a girl can express it, any indication that she does not want to be touched in certain ways needs to be respected. As she grows up, she will express a wish for still more privacy, extending it to activities such as bathing, dressing, or using the bathroom that were previously performed openly in front of parents and siblings. A wish for privacy may also be expressed psychologically by keeping secrets or not wanting to talk about something. Although parents must judge the appropriateness of these requests, no age is too young for a father to begin noticing and respecting his daughter's innate sense of boundaries.

Allow a voice of protest and sharing power within the family. A father imbues his daughter with strength in the world when, over the years, he listens to her, respects her boundaries, and tells her repeatedly that she has the right to speak up without delay whenever she feels her boundaries are being disrespected. A father who gives his daughter the gift of encouraging her to express her *voice of protest* helps her carry her self-respect actively into the world. By teaching her to speak up in protest sooner, rather than later or never, he is reversing the age-old message that silences women and teaches them to absorb demeaning and exploitative treatment.

In order to bestow on her this gift, a father must be prepared to do more than encourage his daughter to protest elsewhere. He must show her, within the family, that when she does so she will not be ignored or punished, but listened to. Challenges to a father's authority must not be considered unacceptable, even if at times they are unreasonable. Sitting down and respectfully discussing with a child of any age the reasons behind a parental decision helps a child to see that even when power is exercised, it is not necessarily exercised arbitrarily.

Moreover, as she grows older, a girl must gradually be given a share of power over her own life. From time to time, at least by adolescence, a father must be willing to back down and concede power to his daughter. Such moments are inevitably difficult for both father and daughter, especially because for an adolescent girl the power conflict may involve issues related to her sexuality. In order to give her power, a father must replace it with trust in his daughter's character. It is a risk that, at the right moments, he must take. If he does not, he will inevitably lose her. More tragically, she will have lost him as a parent, guide, teacher, and example of a man who is willing, out of love and respect, to relinquish his power over her so that she will be equipped to claim her own place in the world.

When she does go into the world beyond the family, she will shape her power relationships with men in the image created by her relationship with her father. The way in which pivotal power conflicts between them were resolved will determine whether she feels she can share in, or must submit to, the power men hold.

Fathers and Sons

A son's attitude toward women will be significantly shaped in childhood by the words and deeds of his father. Even if a father is still trying to resolve difficulties he has with women and sexuality, he can help his son avoid repeating typical patterns of abusive relationship between men and women. A father can begin when his son is very young by attending to the same fundamental issues detailed in the previous section on fathers and daughters. The ability of a parent to listen to a child's experience from an early age, respect his boundaries and privacy, and share power with him are such basic means of conveying respect that they apply equally to the relationship between father and son. But the special kind of work a father can do with his son, in order not to perpetuate the masculine wound that might lead to exploitation of women, focuses on three central issues:

Question the existing masculine myth of the feminine. A father must examine the degree to which he holds his wife and other women responsible for his emotional well-being. To the extent that a man maintains his anger at women for not living up to his myth of what they should provide for him, his son will develop the same anger. A father can try, by word and by deed, to teach his son that women are not his servants, healers, sexual playthings, or tormentors. In rejecting the destructive cultural myth of women, father and son will be in a position to relate to women in new ways.

Show respect for the inner world of the masculine. Any attempt to change the old myth of the feminine immediately throws men back on themselves. A father trapped by his overdependence on the power of the feminine is harming his son by undervaluing what it means to be a man. His son will be deprived of inner resources that are the psychological birthright of all men. The inner world of the masculine has an enormous capacity for creativity, meaning, feeling, self-healing, and self-renewal, which a man can learn to draw upon in his daily life and fall back upon in times of pain and crisis.

    A father can bestow the gift of the inner masculine by letting his son in on the father's inner world. As a son grows, it becomes increasingly important for him to learn what his father is like inside. If he can see that his father can tolerate mixed feelings such as strength and vulnerability, action and reflection, hope and grief, and ambition and sacrifice, a son can begin to strike his own balance in life, instead of relegating to the inner scrap-heap ways of thinking and feeling that do not fit the culturally approved model of the strong, outer-goal–oriented man.

Eventually a father will be called upon to confide his own struggle with issues of sexuality and intimacy. When fathers leave this vital part of their own lives out of their relationships with sons, the sons fall by default into the cultural stereotype that says the women around them will take care of issues that have to do with intimacy. Fathers need not have mastered the mysteries of intimacy in order to tell their sons about their struggles; they have only to talk to their sons about some of their failures, losses, and ongoing conflicts, as well as their triumphs, exciting adventures, and ecstatic moments. Simply showing their sons that they *have* an inner world in which they experience a mixture of feeling states about sexuality and intimacy will create a legacy of masculine strength that diminishes overdependence on women.

Shape a healthy attitude toward sexual fantasy. Because sexual fantasy plays such an important part in men's lives, a father can make a special contribution to his son's psychological development in the way he helps shape the son's attitudes toward the sexual fantasy world. The most important contribution a father can make toward his son's sexual well-being is to draw a sharp line between sexual fantasy and sexual behavior, then to let the son know that his fantasy life, whatever it may be, is a perfectly natural exploration of his inner world and the range of feeling states that life offers. A son who is taught to respect and explore his inner sexual images will be more receptive to evaluating what kinds of behavior are healthy or unhealthy for him. He will be less likely to project his sexual fantasy world onto outer life in ways that can be destructive to him and to others.

A father need not feel he has to share specific sexual fantasies with his son or ask that the son reveal his own. We all retain the right to privacy concerning any images—sexual or otherwise—that emanate from our inner worlds. But disclosing to a son that a father *has* an inner world that includes sexual fantasy can help open the way for him to discover his own inner resources.

Share power with sons.   The issue of power is a difficult one between fathers and sons. Fathers who maintain an autocratic stance in the family are grooming their sons to wield power over others as soon as they get the chance. Deprived of a way to grow gradually toward power sharing with his father, a son is more likely to try instead to gain power over the feminine. There is a diabolical equation at work here: After being deprived of power by his father, the culture tells a man as he matures that the way to earn his power is to assert it over women—usually in ways that include challenging women's sexual boundaries. But we now have the opportunity to look for different ways of sharing power, including bringing women in as equal partners in matters both global and intimate.

Epilogue
The Healing Moment

When a forbidden-zone relationship becomes erotically charged, several moments of decision inevitably occur that determine whether the sexuality will be contained psychologically or acted upon physically. Whenever a man relinquishes his sexual agenda toward his protégée in order to preserve her right to a nonsexual relationship, a healing moment occurs.

Because so many women have been previously injured by the uncontained sexuality of men who have had power over them, the potential healing power of restraint is enormous. Not only is the woman made safe from being exploited by this particular man, but the moment kindles the promise that she can be valued as a woman entirely apart from her sexual value to other men. In these moments life takes a new turn, and injury from the past as well as hopelessness about the future can be healed. It may take many years for the promise of this moment to be realized. Yet innumerable women with whom I have spoken over the years—patients, friends, colleagues—have been able to identify the moment life took this hopeful turn for them, and for many that moment occurred in forbidden-zone relationships when men who had the power to engage them sexually chose not to do so.

For some women the healing moment was explicit, with the sexual possibilities of the forbidden-zone relationship discussed, acknowledged, and relinquished. For other women the subject of sexuality never came up directly; the simple fact that the man never related sexually—at a time the woman knew she was vulnerable to seduction—provided the healing moment.

When a man in power relinquishes his protégée as a potential sexual partner, he also creates a healing moment for himself. In giving her up sexually, he releases both of them from the secret demand that the woman heal him, an underlying psychological reality that permeates so many relationships in which sexual exploitation of the forbidden zone occurs.

At the moment a man releases a woman from this healing demand, he begins to glimpse the possibility that he can recover vast inner resources of his own. These stores of masculine strength are the ones that have been previously denied to him by cultural and family myths that devalue his inner world and encourage the myth that only women, through their sexuality, can provide him with feelings of renewal and aliveness.

The men I know who have experienced these healing moments treasure them as the beginning of a liberation from an endless cycle of sexual pursuit that led to an emptiness that only made them more desperately seek sexual healing from the next woman. Many of these men, whether or not they have ever violated the forbidden zone, report that giving up the quest for sexual healing has been both the most difficult and most rewarding emotional work in their lives. It has brought them an entirely new and deepened sense of self, along with a renewed capacity for a loving relationship with a woman.

A fitting conclusion to this book can be found in the following case example of a forbidden-zone relationship in which both the man and woman experienced a mutual healing moment. Elaine Sewell and George Byner, now law partners in San Francisco, were contributors to the research phase of this book, clarifying certain legal issues raised by sexual exploitation of relationships of trust. But as our consultations evolved, the two of them revealed their own dramatic experience with sex in the forbidden zone.

Elaine, now thirty-four, first met George, forty-six, six years ago when she was assigned as an intern in his firm during her final year of law school. She researched his cases and prepared drafts of legal documents for him. He was impressed with her work, and she with his intellect and his caring attitude toward both her and his clients. Feeling validated by their working relationship, Elaine discovered that many doubts she had harbored about her intellect and competence vanished, and she became excited as never before about work and life.

Elaine disclosed that although she was single, for the first time in her memory she was not focusing on finding a mate and felt free of a depression she had long carried because she was alone. George appeared to have a solid marriage and family life. Their admiration and affection for each other, along with the late evenings they spent together preparing cases, presented many opportunities for flirtation; yet for nearly a year neither of them made any verbal or physical reference to the possibility of sexuality between them.

A crisis occurred before Elaine's graduation. Because her internship with him was ending, George had to decide whether to offer her a position in his firm. But things were no longer so simple. As Elaine subsequently told me:

There was nothing more important to me than getting that job, because it would give me the chance to go on working with George in what was clearly the kind of mentoring relationship that was helping transform my life. And of course I could tell that he was excited by working with me. But I was absolutely convinced that the price of a job would be for me to have an affair with George, and I knew that if that happened it would be psychologically disastrous for me. I would lose all sense of the hope and self-esteem that working with him had given me, because I would always believe that it had been based on sex.

Yet I also knew that if he wanted to have a sexual relationship with me I would not be able to turn him down. I was shocked when I realized I was in a position in which I would have readily agreed to something I knew would damage me. Then again, he had never made any move toward me that was sexual, so another part of me was wondering whether I was making up a sexual drama that wasn't really there.

Despite the wonderful working relationship we had and the exciting possibilities for the future, as the time for a decision came, I was completely confused and in a great deal of pain. It seemed that I would lose either way: If I didn't get the job I would lose my vital connection to George and interpret it as a statement that I was not competent enough; if I did get the job, it would inevitably become tarnished by a sexual relationship.

As George related his side of the story, it became clear that Elaine had not been imagining the sexual tension between them; if anything, she had underestimated it. Behind his professional demeanor, George's feelings for Elaine had placed him in a bind from which he saw no satisfactory way out:

Elaine was absolutely right about what she sensed. I was going through my version of the same thing. I had been having constantly escalating sexual fantasies about her almost from the beginning. First I fell in love with the way her mind worked, but it was hard not to carry it over to the rest of her. I felt some safety in the fact that her year of internship would end, because I felt I could hold out until she left the firm.

But it was clear that, on the merits, she deserved to be hired after her graduation. So I found myself hoping she would leave, just to protect myself. Yet I knew this would be patently unfair and hurtful to her. On the other hand, I very much wanted to hire her, but I felt my motivation was compromised by my wanting her near me because of my sexual feelings. Just as she imagined, I was equally sure that once she worked here I would not be able to resist having a sexual relationship with her. It was torture for me, too, especially because my fantasies about Elaine made me question my marriage in a way that I found unaccountable, because I hadn't previously felt anything was missing with my wife.

This seemingly unresolvable crisis was worked out through a nearly silent and almost imperceptible healing moment. As Elaine recalled:

One night about a week before George had to decide about offering me a job, we were working late together. I asked him what he thought he would do about hiring me. I was so scared to get anywhere near the sexual tension I felt between us that I couldn't even ask him whether he had any reservations about my ability. He just said that he hadn't made up his mind yet.

We were both silent, and our eyes met. For the first time, I thought I could see the pain he was feeling, and something in me longed to take care of it. I felt completely unprotected. In that moment I would have done anything for him, no matter what the consequences. I almost wished he would embrace me just so we could get on with the sexual relationship that seemed so inevitable. I was shocked, but terribly relieved, when George looked away and directed us back to the work we were doing. I didn't think it was possible for a man to turn away from sexual energy of the sort we had going between us. Although I had no idea why he did it, I felt from then on that if I were offered the job, it would be safe to take it and would not be compromised by my having any sexual obligation. When he did not sexually respond to that moment of my greatest vulnerability, it was as if a spell was broken, not just the one I felt with George, but one I felt I had carried since childhood.

George remembers the same moment with the utmost clarity:

I was going crazy with tension that evening. My fantasies were in favor of solving this problem in the generic masculine way: Just take her in your arms and get it over with. I was prepared to do it that way at this point more to resolve the tension than because I felt an overwhelming sexuality.

Then the moment occurred that Elaine described, when she was completely unguarded, obviously ready to go along with me in my sexual scenario. But something else happened. When I saw how unprotected she was, I suddenly realized that Elaine was my spiritual daughter, and I had to treat her that way, no matter how well I could have rationalized that we had a right to have an affair. This meant that I had to give up, not just for this moment, but once and for all, the idea that we would ever have a sexual liaison.

We finished our work that night, and I went home with a feeling different from anything I had felt before, both empty and renewed at the same time. I mourned the loss of the possibility of sex between us for months, but I was able to offer her the job.

In the six years since that moment, George and Elaine have continued to work together creatively and productively. After four years, Elaine became a partner in the firm. She is now engaged, and George's marriage continues to be intact and satisfying. Their relationship does not extend outside the office. But in their day-to-day collaboration, and in the memory of what they went through to gain what they have today, they are both aware that their special connection has yielded gifts neither of them had expected:

> Until that moment with Elaine, I never thought that I would experience anything but loss and deprivation by giving up what my fantasies told me would be a special, magical, sexual meeting. Well, I did feel the loss, but ever since then I have access to a quality of strength and inner satisfaction that I had never known before. Not that everything is blissful. There are still many difficult moments in my marriage, with my children, just with myself. But I trust myself more. And it keeps growing. I feel as if that experience with Elaine relieved me of the illusion men have that women hold the secret cure for us.
>
> Not becoming sexual with her opened a channel of psychological development that I think will last all my life. Not touching her, and realizing that I had to give up the notion of *ever* touching her or anyone else over whom I had that kind of power, was the hardest thing I've ever done in my life. But I sure would like other men to know that it can be done, and that there are great rewards, eventually, on the other side.

For Elaine, that healing moment six years ago lives with equal force:

> For a year after it happened, neither of us referred to the incident. To me it was enough of a gift that it happened, and that we could go on working together. I think we both just had to catch our breath and get our bearings. But I was shaken by the experience. I entered therapy with a woman. She encouraged me to talk to George about the incident, so that he could help me understand his part in it. If I never asked him whether he had had those feelings toward me, I

would be in danger of wondering all my life whether it had been all in my imagination. So after a year I asked him what he had been going through. And he told me. Just the fact that we could talk about it, without risking the danger of reengaging the sexual feelings, showed that our relationship had acquired a whole new dimension. Some friends who have been in intense, long-term therapy are the only ones I can think of who ever had a nonsexual relationship in which this kind of depth and honesty about sexual undercurrents could be talked about safely and constructively, rather than seductively.

What this meant to me, and it has been proven in the years since, is that there is hope for women to heal our incest wounds. That might seem like strong language, but I don't know a woman who isn't somehow injured by the fact that, even without any obvious incest, we have all grown up taking for granted how much our real fathers or other powerful men in our lives have wanted from us. Even if what they want isn't always sexual, even when they want us to be strong and succeed, somehow it feels too much as if we have to do it their way. And this undermines whatever we accomplish, because ultimately we end up feeling that we failed them. Even if we were strong and succeeded, we did it for them, to take care of them, and our self-esteem remains conditional on their approval.

Despite everything else George has done for me, his ability to let go of the sexual agenda released me from the incest pact. I sensed he was giving up something that was extremely hard for him to give up because he saw what the cost would be for me. I sensed it, but a year later it was very important for me to hear him confirm it. It was also important because then I found out all it meant for him, too, and I was glad that he was so rewarded for his sacrifice.

That moment, which freed me from the incest pact, has allowed whatever I have since accomplished, even my failures, to be *mine*. And I'm sure that my ability to have the kind of intimate relationship with a man I have now, which is one of pretty much complete psychological equality, also grew from that healing moment.

Although most of this book has concentrated on documenting the damage done when men in power sexually exploit women, every forbidden-zone relationship in which sexual tension appears also presents an opportunity to heal. Because the man holds the balance of power, it is his responsibility to turn an impending sexual disaster into a healing moment. He must, for her sake, give up his sexual agenda toward her, once and for all. When he does this, he frees both of them to recover the abundant resources of the self.

Healing moments are also available to all of us in our daily lives, in or out of forbidden-zone relationships. No matter how much previous injury we have perpetrated or endured, we have only to look around us each day for an opportunity to take a barely discernible turn in a direction different from the one we are used to taking. The intact, untapped resources inside us are ready to respond when we become ready to call upon them.

Resources

ORGANIZATIONS

The following national organizations have a great deal of experience in sexual exploitation by professionals. They are prepared to listen responsively to your complaint and direct you back toward your own community for obtaining legal help, therapy, or bringing ethical charges against the professional involved.

Walk-In Counseling Center
2421 Chicago Ave. South
Minneapolis, MN 55404
612/870-0565
This center has helped more victims of sexual exploitation by professionals than any other in the country. Referral service and many informational publications are available, notably *Psychotherapist Sexual Involvement with Clients: Intervention and Prevention,* edited by Gary Schoener and colleagues, an extremely comprehensive collection of nationwide resources in the field of exploitation.

I've listed the above organization separately because I think it's extremely important in light of its accomplishments. The remaining organizations, which are also important and helpful, are in alphabetical order.

Association Against Client Exploitation by Professionals
(AACEP)
P.O. Box 533
Havertown, PA 19083
215/449-6663
Membership organization for both victims and interested pro-
fessionals. It offers a newsletter and local and national refer-
ral services.

Association of Psychologically Abused Patients (APAP)
P.O. Box 9682
Ft. Worth, TX 76147
817/732-6565
Provides referrals both locally and nationally.

Center for the Prevention of Sexual and Domestic Violence
(CPSDV)
1914 N. 34th St., Ste. 105
Seattle, WA 98103
206/634-1903
Newsletter and referral services available—special expertise
in clergy abuse. Offers publications by Reverend Marie M.
Fortune, author of *Is Nothing Sacred? When Sex Invades the
Pastoral Relationship.*

Consumers Against Sexual Exploitation (CASE)
5036 N. 56th St.
Milwaukee, WI 53218
414/464-5845
Provides referrals and a publication, *Couched in Silence: An
Advocacy Handbook on Sexual Exploitation in Therapy.*

Stop Abuse by Counselors (STOP ABC)
P.O. Box 68292
Seattle, WA 98168
206/243-2723
Provides nationwide referrals.

Tapestry, Inc.
20 Sacramento St.
Cambridge, MA 02138
617/661-0248
Offers workshops and therapy.

Following are the national organizations for most of the helping professions. Although they exist to represent the interests of their members, they are all capable of receiving ethical complaints and should be able to direct you to a branch of their organization in your area where you can file your complaint or ask for referrals to professionals sensitive to issues of sexual exploitation.

In addition, these organizations will counsel their own members who step forward to address ethical problems they might be having. Both ethics committees and impaired-professionals programs are available to help, and they will look favorably on professionals who voluntarily take some responsibility for their own ethical violations.

American Association for Marriage and Family Therapy (AAMFT)
1717 K St. NW, #407
Washington, DC 20006
202/429-1825

American Association of Pastoral Counselors (AAPC)
9508A Lee Hwy.
Fairfax, VA 22031
703/385-6967

American Association of University Professors (AAUP)
1012 14th St., Ste. 500
Washington, DC 20005
202/737-5900

American Bar Association (ABA)
750 Lake Shore Dr.
Chicago, IL 60611
312/988-5000

American Dental Association (ADA)
211 E. Chicago Ave.
Chicago, IL 60611
312/440-2500

American Medical Association (AMA)
535 N. Dearborn St.
Chicago, IL 60610
312/645-5000

American Nurses Association (ANA)
2420 Pershing Rd.
Kansas City, MO 64108
816/474-5720

American Psychiatric Association (APA)
1400 K St. NW
Washington, DC 20005
202/682-6000

American Psychological Association (APA)
1200 17th St. NW
Washington, DC 20036
202/955-7600

Association of American Colleges (AAC)
Project on the Status of Women
1818 R St. NW
Washington, DC 20009
202/387-3760
Also publishes a newsletter.

Federation of State Medical Boards of the United States
2630 W. Freeway, Ste. 138
Ft. Worth, TX 76102
817/335-1141
Can direct you to your state medical board and provide other information about ethical issues.

National Association of Social Workers (NASW)
7981 Eastern Ave.
Silver Spring, MD 20910
301/565-0333

Following are major religious organizations that also accept ethical complaints and can direct you to services in your area. Religious groups are particularly well prepared to help counsel their own clergy who are having ethical problems.

National Conference of Catholic Bishops
(Catholic churches)
1313 Massachusetts Ave. NW
Washington, DC 20005
202/659-6774

National Council of Churches (Protestant churches)
475 Riverside Dr.
New York, NY 10115
212/870-2200

Union of American Hebrew Congregations (Reform)
838 Fifth Ave.
New York, NY 10021
212/249-0100

Union of Orthodox Jewish Congregations of America
45 West 36th St.
New York, NY 10018
212/563-4000

United Synagogue of America (Conservative)
155 Fifth Ave.
New York, NY 10010
212/533-7800

  The following groups can help you obtain legal assistance:

Center for Women's Studies and Services
2467 E St.
San Diego, CA 92102
619/233-8984

Citizens Against Lawyer Abuse (CALA)
P.O. Box 1881
El Cajon, CA 92020

Legal Advocates for Women (LAW)
320 Clement St.
San Francisco, CA 94118
415/752-9404

National Center for Women and Family Law
799 Broadway, Rm. 402
New York, NY 10003
212/674-8200

National Coalition Against Sexual Assault
The Sexual Violence Center
1222 W. 31st St.
Minneapolis, MN 55408
612/824-2864

National Women's Law Center
1616 P St. NW
Washington, DC 20036
202/328-5160

9 to 5, National Association of Working Women
614 Superior Ave. NW, Rm. 852
Cleveland, OH 44113
216/566-9308

NOW Legal Defense and Education Fund (LDEF)
99 Hudson St.
New York, NY 10013
212/925-6635

Women's Law Project
125 S. 9th St., Ste. 401
Philadelphia, PA 19107
215/928-9801

The following are victims' self-help or advocacy groups.
Many of them also publish newsletters.

Adults Molested as Children United; Parents United;
Sons and Daughters United
P.O. Box 952
San Jose, CA 95168
408/280-5055

Al-Anon
P.O. Box 862, Midtown Station
New York, NY 10018-0862
800/356-9996; 212/245-3151

Association for the Sexually Harassed
220 E. Mermaid Ln., Ste. 119
Philadelphia, PA 19118
215/665-0274

Brother—The National Organization for Changing Men
1660 Broad St.
Cranston, RI 02905
Newsletter available.

The Center for Women Policy Studies
2000 P St. NW
Washington, DC 20036
202/872-1770
Publishes journal *Response* and other publications.

Iowa Coalition Against Sexual Abuse
25th and Carpenter
Illinois Hall
Des Moines, IA 50311

Minnesota Program for Victims of Sexual Assault
300 Bigelow Bldg., 450 N. Syndicate St.
St. Paul, MN 55104
612/642-0256
Newsletter available.

National Organization for Victim Assistance
171 D St. NW
Washington, DC 20004
202/393-NOVA
Newsletter available.

North Dakota Council on Abused Women's Services
418 E. Rosser, #210
Bismarck, ND 58501
Newsletter available.

Oregon Coalition Against Sexual and Domestic Violence
2336 SE Belmont St.
Portland, OR 97214
Newsletter available.

Victims Anonymous
9514–9 Reseda Blvd., #607
Northridge, CA 91324
818/993-1139

Women's Resource Center
P.O. Box 5089
Norman, OK 73070
Newsletter available.

BOOKS

This bibliography has been divided into five sections: Women's Issues and Psychology; Men's Issues and Psychology; Sexual Exploitation, Abuse, and Harassment; Jungian Psychology; and Other Psychology and the Helping Professions. The books listed have enriched my own understanding of sex in the forbidden zone, and I recommend them as sources of both psychological and practical wisdom.

Women's Issues and Psychology

Reading a book can suddenly awaken us to a new level of consciousness that will allow us to reshape our lives. The books in this section have had exactly that effect on me and on many women and men I have known as patients, colleagues, and friends. Especially noteworthy are those by Bradley, Gilligan, Harding, Leonard, Norwood, Washbourn, and Woodman. The others are classics that define the vision of modern feminine psychology.

Belenky, Mary Field, et al. *Women's Ways of Knowing: The Development of Self, Voice and Mind.* New York: Basic Books, 1986.

Bolen, Jean Shinoda. *Goddesses in Everywoman: A New Psychology of Women.* San Francisco: Harper & Row, 1984.

Bradley, Marion Zimmer. *The Mists of Avalon.* New York: Alfred A. Knopf, 1983.

Chesler, Phyllis. *Women and Madness.* New York: Avon Books, 1973.

Demetrakopoulos, Stephanie. *Listening to Our Bodies: The Rebirth of Feminine Wisdom.* Boston: Beacon Press, 1983.

Gilligan, Carol. *In a Different Voice: Psychological Theory and Women's Development.* Cambridge: Harvard University Press, 1982.

Harding, M. Esther. *The Way of All Women.* New York: G. P. Putnam's Sons, 1970.

_____. *Women's Mysteries: Ancient and Modern.* New York: Bantam, 1973.

Leonard, Linda Schierse. *The Wounded Woman: Healing the Father-Daughter Relationship.* Boston: Shambhala, 1983.

_____. *On the Way to the Wedding: Transforming the Love Relationship.* Boston: Shambhala, 1986.

Miller, Jean Baker. *Toward a New Psychology of Women.* Boston: Beacon Press, 1986.

Miller, Sue. *The Good Mother.* New York: Harper & Row, 1986.

Norwood, Robin. *Women Who Love Too Much.* Los Angeles: Jeremy P. Tarcher, 1986.

Perera, Sylvia Brinton. *Descent to the Goddess: A Way of Initiation for Women.* Toronto: Inner City Books, 1981.

Washbourn, Penelope. *Becoming Woman: The Quest for Wholeness in Female Experience.* New York: Harper & Row, 1977.

Woodman, Marian. *Addiction to Perfection: The Still Unravished Bride.* Toronto: Inner City Books, 1982.

_____. *The Pregnant Virgin.* Toronto: Inner City Books, 1985.

Men's Issues and Psychology

Any of these books will profoundly inform both men and women about what lies beneath the surface of men's sexual struggles. My personal favorite is the book by Henderson, a mentor who has never failed me and who in his ninth decade continually amazes by vigorously providing a model of the best a man may become.

Bolen, Jean Shinoda. *Gods in Everyman: A New Psychology of Men's Lives and Loves.* San Francisco: Harper & Row, 1989.

Colman, Arthur, and Libby Colman. *The Father: Mythology and Changing Roles.* Wilmette, Ill.: Chiron, 1988.

Henderson, Joseph L. *Thresholds of Initiation.* Middletown, Conn.: Wesleyan University Press, 1967.

Johnson, Robert A. *He: Understanding Masculine Psychology.* New York: Perennial Library, 1977.

Levinson, Daniel. *The Seasons of a Man's Life.* New York: Ballantine Books, 1978.

Monick, Eugene. *Phallos: Sacred Image of the Masculine.* Toronto: Inner City Books, 1987.

Pruett, Kyle D. *The Nurturing Father: Journey Toward the Complete Man.* New York: Warner Books, 1987.

Trachtenberg, Peter. *The Casanova Complex: Compulsive Lovers and Their Women.* New York: Poseidon Press, 1988.

Tyrrell, Thomas J. *Urgent Longings: Reflections on the Experience of Infatuation, Human Intimacy and Contemplative Love.* Whitinsville, Mass.: Affirmation Books, 1980.

Sexual Exploitation, Abuse, and Harassment

The book by Schoener and colleagues, in press as of this writing, promises to serve as a virtual encyclopedia of resources about sexual exploitation for both professionals and clients. Herman's work on incest is already a classic that lays the groundwork for understanding many aspects of sexual abuse. Fortune's book breaks new ground in dealing with sexual abuse by pastors. The publications by Bates, Burgess, Gabbard, and Pope serve as important resources that detail the field of professional abuse and will be especially valuable to professionals who deal with previously exploited patients or clients. These books contain excellent bibliographies referencing the professional literature on this subject.

Bates, Carolyn M., and Annette M. Brodsky. *Sex in the Therapy Hour: A Case of Professional Incest.* New York: Guilford Press, 1989.

Brownmiller, Susan. *Against Our Will: Men, Women and Rape.* New York: Bantam Books, 1976.

Burgess, Ann W., and Carol R. Hartman, eds. *Sexual Exploitation of Patients by Health Professionals.* New York: Praeger, 1986.

Dziech, Billie Wright, and Linda Weiner. *The Lecherous Professor: Sexual Harassment on Campus.* Boston: Beacon Press, 1984.

Farley, Lin. *Sexual Shakedown: The Sexual Harassment of Women on the Job.* New York: Warner Books, 1980.

Fortune, Marie M., *Is Nothing Sacred? When Sex Invades the Pastoral Relationship.* San Francisco: Harper & Row, 1989.

Freeman, Lucy, and Julie Roy. *Betrayal: The True Story of the First Woman to Successfully Sue Her Psychiatrist for Using Sex in the Guise of Therapy.* New York: Stein and Day, 1976.

Gabbard, Glen O., ed. *Sexual Exploitation in Professional Relationships.* Washington, D.C.: American Psychiatric Press, 1989.

Herman, Judith Lewis. *Father-Daughter Incest.* Cambridge: Harvard University Press, 1981.

Howell, Elizabeth, and Marjorie Bayes. *Women and Mental Health.* New York: Basic Books, 1981.

MacKinnon, Catharine A. *Sexual Harassment of Working Women.* New Haven: Yale University Press, 1979.

Plasil, Ellen. *Therapist: The Shocking Autobiography of a Woman Sexually Exploited by Her Analyst.* New York: St. Martin's/Marek, 1985.

Pope, Kenneth S., and Jacqueline Bouhoutsos. *Sexual Intimacy Between Therapists and Patients.* New York: Praeger, 1986.

Schoener, Gary, Jeanette Milgrom, John Gonsiorek, Ellen Luepker, and Ray Conroe, eds. *Psychotherapist Sexual Involvement with Clients: Intervention and Prevention.* Minneapolis: Walk-In Counseling Center (2421 Chicago Ave. South, Minneapolis, MN 55404), 1989.

Stone, Alan A. *Law, Psychiatry, and Morality.* Washington, D.C.: American Psychiatric Press, 1984.

Walker, E., and T. D. Young. *A Killing Cure.* New York: Henry Holt, 1986.

Weissberg, Michael. *Dangerous Secrets: Maladaptive Responses to Stress.* New York: W. W. Norton, 1983.

White, William L. *Incest in the Organizational Family: The Ecology of Burnout in Closed Systems.* Bloomington, Ill.: Lighthouse Training Institute, 1986.

Jungian Psychology

Jung is important as a pioneer of modern psychology and as a historical figure whose own sexual relationships have cast a long shadow, but it is a shadow to which we have been given access. Biographical material alluding to these matters and more can be found in the books by Carotenuto, Hannah, and Jensen.

The best books about Jungian psychology are by Jung himself; they are incomparable in the way they bring to life all the richness and healing potential that lie inside us. His autobiography, *Memories, Dreams, Reflections,* also serves as an introduction to his ideas, as does *Two Essays.* Everything mentioned in this book about the interplay of erotic forces that occurs, invisibly, between two people in a closed room is built upon Jung's description of this process in *The Psychology of the Transference.*

Carotenuto, Aldo. *A Secret Symmetry: Sabina Spielrein Between Jung and Freud.* New York: Pantheon Books, 1982.

Hannah, Barbara. *Jung: His Life and Work.* New York: G. P. Putnam's Sons, 1976.

Jensen, Ferne, ed. *C. G. Jung, Emma Jung and Toni Wolff: A Collection of Remembrances.* San Francisco: Analytical Psychology Club, 1982.

Jung, C. G. *Memories, Dreams, Reflections.* New York: Vintage, 1963.

_____. *The Psychology of the Transference.* Princeton: Princeton/Bollingen, 1969.

————. *Two Essays on Analytical Psychology.* Princeton: Princeton/Bollingen, 1972.

Jung, C. G., et al. *Man and His Symbols.* New York: Doubleday, 1964.

Other Psychology and the Helping Professions

Miller's books have rapidly become classics that allow both therapists and patients to understand with great clarity patterns of psychological abuse from childhood that had heretofore remained hidden. The other books listed provide valuable perspectives for people in the helping professions in dealing with the abuses of power.

Copans, Stuart, and Thomas Singer. *Who's the Patient Here? Portraits of the Young Psychotherapist.* New York: Oxford University Press, 1978.

Edelwich, Jerry. *Sexual Dilemmas for the Helping Professional.* New York: Brunner/Mazel, 1982.

Fromm-Reichmann, Frieda. *Principles of Intensive Psychotherapy.* Chicago: Phoenix Books, 1960.

Guggenbühl-Craig, Adolf. *Power in the Helping Professions.* Dallas: Spring Publications, 1971.

Kilburg, R., P. Nathan, and C. Thoreson. *Professionals in Distress: Issues, Syndromes, and Solutions in Psychology.* Washington, D.C.: American Psychological Association, 1986.

Kottler, Jeffrey A. *On Being a Therapist.* San Francisco: Jossey-Bass, 1987.

Masson, Jeffrey Mousaieff. *The Assault on Truth: Freud's Suppression of the Seduction Theory.* New York: Farrar Straus Giroux, 1984.

Miller, Alice. *Prisoners of Childhood: The Drama of the Gifted Child and the Search for the True Self.* New York: Basic Books, 1981.

———. *For Your Own Good: Hidden Cruelty in Child-Rearing and the Roots of Violence.* New York: Farrar Straus Giroux, 1983.

———. *Thou Shalt Not Be Aware: Society's Betrayal of the Child.* New York: New American Library, 1986.

Schwebel, M., J. Skorina, and G. Schoener. *Assisting Impaired Psychologists.* Washington, D.C.: American Psychological Association, 1988.